WHY WE LOVE TEA

A TEA LOVER'S GUIDE TO TEA RITUALS, HISTORY, AND CULTURE

...THERE CAME A KNOCK AT THE DOOR, AND THE BUTLER ENTERED WITH A
LADEN TEA-TRAY AND SET IT DOWN UPON A SMALL JAPANESE TABLE. THERE WAS
A RATTLE OF CUPS AND SAUCERS AND THE HISSING OF A FLUTED GEORGIAN
URN. TWO GLOBE-SHAPED CHINA DISHES WERE BROUGHT IN BY A PAGE.
DORIAN GRAY WENT OVER AND POURED OUT THE TEA.

Oscar Wilde

from *The Picture of Dorian Gray*

mango
PUBLISHING GROUP

Project editor VALERIA MANFERTO DE FABIANIS

Editorial assistant LAURA ACCOMAZZO

Graphic layout CLARA ZANOTTI

PHOTOS BY FABIO PETRONI

TEXTS BY GABRIELLA LOMBARDI

RECIPES BY CHEF GIOVANNI RUGGIERI

CONTENTS

FERMENTED (OR BLACK) TEA

PROCESSED TEAS
SCENTED, FLAVORED, AND BLOOMING TEAS

TEA TIME AND
SERVING SUGGESTIONS
20 RECIPES BY CHEF GIOVANNI RUGGIERI

FOREWORD

Before I became a tea lover, I was an avid coffee drinker who dismissed all forms of tea, whether served in cafes or prepared at home. Then, I discovered pure tea leaves, and it was a revelation. I fell deeply in love with this drink and its rituals, primarily for its ever-changing fragrances. I savor these fragrances every time I visit a tea production area or taste the latest crops, which are never the same as the previous ones. I adore the feeling of understanding the spirit of a place from the first few sips and the atmosphere of hospitality and conviviality that a cup of tea fosters, encouraging people to pause for a moment, chat, and share their thoughts.

Tea takes you on a journey of discovery into the rites and cultures of distant lands, and a lifetime is simply not enough to become fully acquainted with this extraordinary drink.

While traveling abroad, I realized that tea is very much in vogue, despite being considered somewhat outdated in Italy. The desire to spread the word about its contemporary allure has been ignited by my encounters with two professionals who share my vision. The result is this book, which embodies the pure and refined aesthetics that align with my interpretation of the tea universe, conveyed through beautiful images and haute cuisine dishes.

Many words have been used to describe the multifaceted world of tea. The primary goal of this work is to clarify the many inaccuracies and conflicting information surrounding tea, starting with its complex terminology. The objective, therefore, is to provide simple and intuitive, yet accurate and precise information about tea, while also piquing the curiosity and interest of anyone looking to explore pure teas: enthusiasts, connoisseurs, industry insiders, and perhaps even newcomers.

After a brief history, we will delve into the botanical and chemical aspects of tea, as well as its health properties. We will also provide insights into various preparation techniques and the ideal accessories required for each method. Even the finest tea, when prepared incorrectly, cannot achieve its full potential, which is why we have focused on traditional, tried-and-true preparation methods. While taste is subjective, the correct preparation method can be learned and serves as the essential standard for evaluating tea quality.

Each tea family offers exceptional products. The pages of this book are an invitation to discover the finest crus that everyone should taste at least once in their lifetime.

As the tea ritual is all about pleasure, you will also find the best foods to pair with each tea variety, as well as delectable recipes featuring tea leaves, extending the delights of this drink from the cup to the plate.

Finally, I must confess that I have written this book in the hope that people will stop telling me, "I don't like tea." I am convinced that there is the right tea for everyone, capable of opening up a new world of sensations. I invite you to find the tea that's right for you – the one that you too will fall in love with.

FOREWORD

13

THE ORIGINS OF TEA

The history of tea is ancient, and legends surrounding its origins abound in every country. Perhaps the most famous is the Chinese tale of Emperor Shen Nong, the father of agriculture and medicine, who maintained strict hygiene and consumed only boiling water. One fateful day in 2737 BC, while boiling water, leaves from a nearby tea shrub were carried by the wind into the cauldron, imparting a golden hue to the water. Intrigued, the emperor exclaimed, "That which Heaven sends brings harmony to our souls." He sampled the resulting brew, and thus, the tea beverage was born.

For the Indians, tea was discovered by Bodhidharma, the son of Kosjuwo, the King of the Indies. Prince Bodhidharma, who had converted to Buddhism, journeyed to China to spread the teachings. After vowing not to sleep for seven years during his meditation, he succumbed to fatigue after the initial five years. To stay awake, he began chewing leaves from a shrub, which acted as a stimulant. These, of course, were tea leaves.

According to Japanese Buddhists, a different legend prevails. After three years of wakefulness, Bodhidharma fell into a deep slumber and dreamt of the women he had loved in his youth. Upon awakening, he was filled with self-disgust and promptly severed his own eyelids. He discarded the eyelids, and from them sprouted a wild shrub whose leaves yielded an extraordinary drink, capable of granting strength and aiding in prolonged meditation.

Putting aside these legends, tea stands as one of China's most significant contributions to humanity and civilization. China undeniably serves as the birthplace of the tea plant, with the Chinese people being the first to discover and utilize it. Throughout the centuries, the tradition of tea consumption has given rise to an extensive industry and a refined, diverse culture that has spread worldwide. The history of tea is lengthy and intricate, deserving of an entire treatise. In this overview, we shall restrict ourselves to a concise exploration, tracing the key phases in the dissemination and use of tea in China.

ANCIENT TIMES AND THE EARLIEST DYNASTIES: THE DAWNING OF TEA

Tea has been a part of Chinese culture since ancient times. The leaves of the tea plant, native to the region bordering China, Laos, and Myanmar, served as a bitter medicinal herb between the eleventh and eighth centuries BC, as evidenced by early sources that refer to the ancient term "tu" for the tea plant as a healing remedy. The Chinese regard the Xishuangbanna area in Yunnan as the birthplace of tea, where many wild tea plants can still be found today. The first tea plantations were established in the fourth century AD in Yunnan and Sichuan.

Initially, tea was primarily consumed as a beverage in the ancient Ba-Shu region of southwest China. As trade and cultural exchanges intensified, the practice of tea-drinking gradually spread along the Yangtze River and into the Central Plains. Tea culture made its initial, subtle appearance during the Wei and Jin dynasties, as well as the Southern and Northern Dynasties, when increased economic and cultural exchanges and the unification of the north and south expanded its consumption further north.

During the ancient Han Dynasty (206 BC - 220 AD), the provinces of Changsha, Hunan, and Chaling emerged as key centers for tea production.

THE TANG DYNASTY: THE BIRTH OF TEA CULTURE

The formidable Tang dynasty (618-907) was marked by a robust economy and a flourishing culture. According to historians, during this era, tea became an integral part of daily life and continued to thrive under the subsequent Song dynasty.

Notably, during the Tang dynasty, tea gained popularity in northern regions of the country as well. This development can be attributed to the rise and spread of the Chan Buddhist sect. Followers of this sect refrained from eating and sleeping at night but were allowed to consume tea. As the sect's following grew, this practice became ingrained. Another reason for the flourishing tea culture during this period was the tradition of offering tea as a tribute to the emperor. This era also witnessed the publication of the first dedicated book on tea, the renowned "The Classic of Tea" by Lu Yu, a landmark event in the establishment of tea culture.

Lu Yu (733-804), revered as the god of tea, offered a comprehensive exploration of tea's origins, history, production, processing, infusion, and tasting. He based his work on the teachings of his predecessors and the extensive research to which he devoted his life, elevating tea tasting to an art form.

During this time, a wide variety of teas existed. Typically, they were produced in round "cakes," and the beverage was commonly prepared through boiling. Moreover, the Tang imperial court began to introduce appealing tea preparation and serving sets.

In 641, Princess Wencheng brought tea to Tibet as part of her dowry. From that moment, tea began to be sold in large quantities on the Chinese border and was introduced in the northeast and southeast as a valuable commodity. Tea started to be traded in exchange for horses, a practice that persisted for over a millennium, spanning the Tang, Song, Ming, and Qing dynasties. The Tibetans, who inhabited a high plain and subsisted primarily on butter, beef, and mutton, readily purchased tea to aid digestion and stay warm. Tibet did not produce tea, which was abundant in the Chinese plains; conversely, horses were scarce. The ancient Tea-Horse Road facilitated the continuous transportation of mules, horses, furs, and medicinal products from Tibet, Sichuan, and Yunnan on one side, and goods from the Chinese plains, including tea, clothing, salt, and everyday items, on the other.

THE SONG DYNASTY: THE ZENITH OF TEA CULTURE

The Song dynasty (960-1279) marked the pinnacle of a highly refined tea culture characterized by elegance and luxury. During this era, there was a shift in emphasis from military to civil affairs, leading to the flourishing of a cultivated intellectual class that produced numerous literary works on the art of tea. Emperor Hui Zong, also known as Zhao Ji (1082-1135), authored the famous "Treatise on Tea" (Da Guan Cha Lu), which stands as the most comprehensive and authoritative account of the sophisticated tea ceremony that was in vogue during the Song Dynasty.

Furthermore, the method of preparing tea evolved from the boiling technique typical of the Tang dynasty to infusion, a method that required both artistic finesse and technical skill. Tea powder was carefully placed in a bowl, boiling water was poured over it, and a specialized "brush" was employed for stirring.

Song-era tea was distinguished by its round bundles, known as dragon and phoenix tea cakes. The production of these cakes expanded to such an extent that as many as 4,000 varieties emerged.

Another distinctive feature of this period was the rise of competitions in the art of tea preparation and presentation, which gained universal popularity among aristocrats, scholars, and common folk alike. The popularity of these competitions spurred a vibrant production of tea pottery, including the black-glazed cups typically used during the tea ceremony.

Tea houses thrived during this era. Tea had become not only an economically and culturally prosperous commodity but also an integral part of everyday life. Some tea houses traded not only in tea but also in dresses and paintings, and they were adorned with flowers and artworks by renowned artists. During the Southern Song dynasty, Japanese monks Enni Bern'en and Nanpo Jomin studied Buddhism in Zhejiang, respectively, in 1235 and 1259. Upon returning to their homeland, they brought back tea seeds and the principles of tea service.

Eisai, a prominent Japanese monk, also journeyed to China to study Buddhist scriptures, first in 1169 and then again in 1187. He, too, returned to Japan with tea seeds and the art of tea making. Eisai later penned a book titled *Kicha Yojoki* (How to Stay Healthy by Drinking Tea), which became the first Japanese book dedicated to tea. To this day, the Japanese tea ceremony, Cha No Yu, is based on the tea powder and brush technique that was prevalent during the Song Dynasty.

THE MING DYNASTY: TEA CULTURE AND A RETURN TO SIMPLICITY

During the Ming dynasty (1368-1644), the art of tea tasting underwent significant transformations. The traditional practice of boiling or infusing tea powder, which had been in use since the Tang and Song dynasties, gave way to the infusion of tea leaves in boiling water. In 1391, Emperor Zhu Yuanzhang issued a decree allowing loose tea to be presented as tribute in place of tea cakes. This shift was driven by an increasing appreciation for the simplicity of loose tea and its ability to preserve the natural flavor of tea.

Tea competitions, once in vogue, began to wane in popularity, and as powdered tea leaves fell out of use, accessories such as metal or stone mortars, stoves, and brushes were discarded in favor of terracotta and porcelain teapots. Notably, a particularly fine and porous clay, rich in iron, was discovered during the middle of the Ming dynasty in Fixing, in the Jiangsu province. Since then, the best teapots have been crafted from this clay, which serves to enhance the natural flavor of tea.

The Ming dynasty marked the apex of monarchical absolutism and centralized power, making it difficult for many intellectuals and artists to express their talents openly. Consequently, they turned to alternative pursuits such as travel, music, chess, painting, and calligraphy, all of which harmoniously coexisted with tea-drinking. Many tea connoisseurs during the Ming dynasty were, in fact, distinguished scholars who authored more than fifty books on tea. Many of these works have been passed down through the generations, contributing to the rich heritage of tea knowledge.

THE QING DYNASTY: TEA'S POPULAR DIMENSION

During the initial phase of the Qing dynasty (1644-1911), tea made its way across the globe. Chinese tea exports surged, reaching a peak production of 134 million kilograms (approximately 301.5 million pounds) in 1886. Chinese tea had gained a firm grip on the world market. However, in the following years, exports experienced a sharp decline as China lost its overseas markets in India, Sri Lanka, Indonesia, and Japan, where local tea cultivation had taken hold.

Throughout the Qing dynasty, Chinese tea culture became an integral part of family life. Gradually, the Chinese tea ceremony also found its way into the Western world, gaining popularity.

The era witnessed a proliferation of tea houses, and the practice of tea-drinking became exceptionally widespread. Public tea houses played a central role in the daily lives of both rural and urban Chinese citizens, serving as meeting places and centers of entertainment. This gave rise to a remarkable and diverse tea house culture.

Furthermore, numerous specialized tea shops began to emerge.

In the early twentieth century, the regions of Jiangxi, Anhui, and Zhejiang experienced a significant boost in the tea industry, with the development of new tea cultivation and processing techniques.

In 1940, the Agricultural College of Fudan University in Shanghai established a department dedicated to tea studies and launched the first specialized tea training course.

THE SPREAD OF TEA IN EUROPE

The introduction of tea to Europe remains shrouded in uncertainty, with debates over whether the Portuguese or the Dutch can claim the distinction. The Portuguese were the first to encounter this novel beverage, but they were financially reliant on the Dutch, who held the reins as the primary importers of goods from the East.

Initially, tea found its way into the holds of Dutch ships, filling the empty spaces left by other cargo. However, it wasn't until 1637 that the Dutch East India Company recognized the profit potential of tea. Soon enough, the Dutch themselves became avid enthusiasts of this new drink. Gradually, the popularity of tea began to spread to Germany and France. Word about this exotic Eastern beverage and its associated health benefits also made its way to England, where it was warmly embraced.

In Russia, tea had been in use since 1567, imported from China through caravan routes. The country even developed its own unique method for preparing tea, involving the use of the samovar.

The arrival of tea in America occurred in the mid-1600s, when the Dutch established New Amsterdam, now known as New York.

Italy, on the other hand, is believed to have been introduced to tea by the Bersaglieri veterans of the Crimean War in 1855.

THE TEA PLANT

BOTANICS, VARIETIES, CULTIVATION, HARVESTS,
AND DIFFUSION

A century later, Robert Fortune discovered that all teas derive from a single plant: an evergreen shrub called Camellia sinensis (L.) O. Kuntze.

We are accustomed to thinking of the tea plant as a shrub. However, if it is not pruned, it can grow as tall as approximately 33-49 feet (10-15 meters). In Yunnan, there are many age-old tea trees, with the oldest dating back 2,700-3,200 years. Ancient Chinese historical records reveal that the leaves of the wild tea plant were initially used for medicinal purposes. The first plantations, in Yunnan and Sichuan, were established in the fourth century AD. From then on, the plant was "tamed," transforming it from a tall tree into a shrub for ease of harvesting. The pruned plant takes the form of a bush-shaped woody shrub, optimizing the crown, thus maximizing the number of leaves available. Indeed, by pruning the top buds, the plant grows outwards rather than upwards. The leaf tea is simple and symmetrical, either oval or lance-shaped, with serrated edges and a midrib. The tea plant reproduces through seeds or cuttings. In the past, the plants were grown naturally from seeds, but nowadays cuttings are preferred.

A cutting has an identical DNA to that of the parent plant. Every seed, on the other hand, is different from the next, and therefore every new plant will have a different genetic makeup from that of the parent plant. When a parent plant, i.e., a plant that grows directly from a seed, produces top-rate tea, it is used to create cuttings. Cloning plants that resist certain climatic conditions and pest attacks, or simply the most productive ones or those that produce high-quality teas, guarantees consistent levels of production. Tea cuttings are shoots of a parent plant that are removed and placed in soil until the roots sprout. When the new plants have reached a height of around 8 inches (15-20 cm), they are ready to be planted.

In southern China, as we have seen, the tea plant has grown naturally since ancient times, thanks to favorable weather conditions. The natural environment surrounding young tea plants profoundly influences their quality. The flavor of tea will vary by changing just one of the fundamental elements, such as soil, water, climate, and sun exposure. The plants that grow in tropical and subtropical regions marked by a mild climate, and the optimal proportion of humidity, rain, and sun, produce the highest quality teas. The tea plant requires well-drained acidic soil and a rainy, cloudy, foggy, and mildly sunny climate. The best teas are produced in the mountains, where the plantations enjoy the best conditions for growth. These teas are appreciated for their freshness and their lingering aromatic notes, suitable for multiple infusions. For plain-growing teas, it is important to shade the plants, creating optimal undergrowth conditions for their growth. Tea quality also depends on the harvest season. Spring is by far the best. At this time, the buds are dark green, smooth, full-bodied, and have good water content, rich in aromas and highly antioxidant and nutritional substances. There are hundreds of botanical specimens of Camellia Sinensis. Indeed, a Chinese proverb says that we can count the stars in the sky, but we cannot give a name to every tea. These specimens are classified in several ways, in addition to the six macro-families split by color classification (green, white, yellow, blue-green, red, and black). For example, they can be classified by harvest season into spring, summer, and autumn teas.

They can be defined as mountain or plain teas, depending on where they were cultivated. Moreover, harvesting may be manual or mechanical, although a manual harvest enables the selection of the best shoots and leaves. The tea plant, like other tropical plants, alternates stages of growth and rest. Shoots sprout during the growth stages, and these are carefully harvested and processed. Unlike for other intensive farming crops, only the leaves of the tea plant are picked, ignoring fruits, flowers, or seeds. In Japan, tea is harvested four times a year. The warmer and more constant climate of Africa, instead, permits continuous harvesting throughout the year.

There are various types of harvesting methods chosen by the producer, which determine the quality of the end product:

- Just the shoot.
- The shoot and one leaf.
- The shoot and two leaves.
- The shoot and three leaves.
- The shoot and four leaves.
- The shoot and five leaves.

Mechanical or semi-mechanical harvesting is widespread in countries where labor costs are high (such as Japan) or where standard or poor-quality tea reserved for tea bags is produced on a large scale (the "crush, tear, and curl" method practiced mainly in India).

THE CHEMISTRY OF TEA

Depending on the chemical reactions undergone by the leaves during processing, tea is classified as:

- Non-oxidized (green tea).
- Oxidized (white, yellow, blue-green, and red tea).
- Fermented (black Chinese teas and Pu'er teas).

Oxidation is a chemical reaction that takes place in the presence of oxygen. Fermentation, unlike oxidation, occurs through the presence of yeasts and bacteria on the tea leaves.

Tea contains various components, including:

- Catechins (green tea is high in ECGC, powerful antioxidants that combat the free radicals responsible for aging and some degenerative diseases).
- Oxidized polyphenols (the theaflavins and thearubigins present in fully oxidized teas; these provide a lower level of protection than catechins).
- Alkaloids (caffeine, theobromine, and theophylline, substances that alter brain function, improve concentration and digestion, and have diuretic and vasodilatory properties; caffeine is released more slowly in tea than in coffee because it tends to bind to the polyphenols - which is why coffee is considered a stimulant, while tea is considered more invigorating and refreshing).
- Amino acids (the protein components required for cell renewal).
- Water, sugars, and essential vitamins such as A, B, C, E, and K.
- Minerals (such as calcium, magnesium, manganese, potassium, fluorine, and zinc).
- Glucosides (substances that give rise to essential oils, providing the aromatic notes of tea).

THE TEA PLANT

THE HEALTH BENEFITS OF TEA

Traditional Chinese medicine recommends drinking at least 3 cups of tea a day to maintain good health.

Recent international studies, presented in New York on September 19, 2012, during the "5th International Scientific Symposium on Tea & Human Health," reveal the health-giving properties of the main substances contained in tea.

In particular, polyphenols are powerful antioxidants, fighting cell damage caused by the free radicals produced as part of normal cell metabolism or as a result of stressful events (radiation, smoke, pollution, UV rays, emotional and physical stress, chemical additives, bacterial and viral attacks, etc.).

Although tea cannot replace fruits and vegetables in the diet, science shows that its leaves contain a higher concentration of antioxidants than most products rich in these molecules. The antioxidant activity of two cups of tea is equal to seven glasses of orange juice, five medium-sized onions, or four medium-sized apples.

More specifically, polyphenols:
- Have anti-cancer properties; tea drinkers are less likely to develop cancer than non-tea drinkers.
- Are powerful anti-inflammatories that play a preventive role against the risk of cardiovascular disease, particularly heart disease and stroke.
- Neutralize free radicals due to their antioxidant properties.
- Stimulate metabolism by decreasing the absorption of fat and favoring weight management.
- Lower cholesterol and sugar levels in the blood.
- Boost the immune system.
- Play a role in preventing the loss of bone mass.
- Decrease the general and lung damage caused by cigarette smoke.
- Protect teeth against cavities.
- Shield the skin against damage caused by sun rays.
- Have an anti-inflammatory effect on the digestive system and intestinal tract.

Caffeine and other substances that stimulate the central nervous system also have beneficial effects on the human body. In particular, they:
- Stimulate concentration.
- Aid digestion and diuresis.

Regarding amino acids, L-Theanine reduces stress and anxiety responses associated with premenstrual syndrome. Recent studies have shown that L-Theanine increases concentration and relaxation and improves sleep disorders.

THE COLORS OF TEA

COLOR CLASSIFICATION OF TEA

For a long time, especially in the West, it was believed that green and black tea came from two distinct plants. In reality, there is just one tea plant, known as Camellia Sinensis, while the various types of tea available stem from factors such as local climatic conditions, harvesting methods, and processing techniques.

In China, tea is traditionally classified into six families, based on the color taken on by the leaves and liquor after processing. According to this color classification, tea can be divided into the following macro-categories:

GREEN TEAS

WHITE TEAS

YELLOW TEAS

BLUE-GREEN TEAS

RED TEAS

BLACK TEAS

Each of these categories includes a wide variety of significantly different products, encompassing a world of unique sensory experiences just waiting to be discovered.

Indeed, these six families are to be considered general categories, comparable in the West to the distinction between red, white, and rosé wines.

QUALITY ASSESSMENT: TEA CLASSIFICATIONS AND TERMS

Over 3,000 types of tea are produced worldwide, and these differ based on the processing method adopted. In this book, we will describe the production techniques specific to each family. Regarding the classification of finished products, in this chapter, we provide an overview of the assessment methods, terms, and acronyms used to evaluate tea quality.

Tea is typically assessed by visually examining the appearance and color of the infusion, and by sampling its flavor, fragrance, and aroma. The appearance is evaluated in terms of strength or delicacy, color and brilliance, purity or impurity.

Once the tea leaves have undergone the full processing cycle and have been dried, experts classify them based on their appearance and type. The first significant distinction, based on the appearance of the leaves, is as follows: leaf quality (full leaves), broken quality (broken leaves), and fanning quality (roughly chopped leaves, generally used for tea bags).

It is essential for the leaves or leaf pieces used for a particular tea variety to be of the same size. This is because during infusion, the leaves release a different aroma, color, and intensity depending on their size. The smaller the leaf, the faster the required infusion time; conversely, the bigger the leaf, the longer the infusion time.

Several terms, designed to create an international parameter of assessment, are used for leaf categories.

FOP: *Flowery Orange Pekoe*

Indicates tea made using the last shoot and the first leaf below it. Young, tender leaves guarantee high-quality tea.

GFOP: *Golden Flowery Orange Pekoe*

FOP varieties added to with golden tips, i.e., the slender, yellow-golden tips of the shoots.

TGFOP: *Tippy Golden Flowery Orange Pekoe*

FOP varieties with a greater percentage of golden tips.

FTGFOP: *Finest Tippy Golden Flowery Orange Pekoe*

Top-rate FOP varieties.

SFTGFOP: *Special Finest Tippy Golden Flowery Orange Pekoe.*

The best FOP varieties.

These acronyms can also be followed by the number 1, indicating first-rate quality (e.g., FTGFOP1).

The letter B before OP indicates broken tea.

Chopped tea leaves are indicated by the letter F(*fanning*).

Finally, leaves under 0.05 inches (1.5 mm) in size are classified as dust and are produced using the *Crushing, Tearing, and Curling method.*

The intrinsic nature of a specific tea quality is judged based on the color, perfume, and flavor of the infusion. The first step is to observe the infusion to identify the type, or "color." The subsequent stage is the olfactory assessment to identify the type, intensity, and persistence of the tea. Finally, flavor is assessed, identifying whether it is rich or delicate, full-bodied or thin, ripe or unripe, fresh or stale.

The leaves are first observed in their dried state and then once infused to assess their tenderness, color, brilliance, and uniformity. Experts then determine and quantify the value of the tea through both their senses and a variety of technical instruments, such as saucers, cups, and bowls, following a well-defined procedure described in the chapter dedicated to professional tasting.

THE ART OF TEA MAKING

A COMPARISON BETWEEN EUROPEAN AND EASTERN INFUSIONS

When discussing the art of tea making, the most common questions are: "how much" and "how long?" As we will see below, these are difficult questions to answer because several different factors must be considered in preparing a good cup of tea.

There are two major tea-making traditions worldwide: the Chinese and the Anglo-Saxon.

The basic principles of these two schools can be summarized as follows:
• Anglo-Saxon, or Western method: a small amount of tea leaves, a long infusion time, and a single infusion.
• Chinese, or Eastern method: a larger quantity of tea leaves, a very short infusion time, and multiple infusions.

As we will explore, it's not a matter of one method being superior to the other, but rather the characteristics of different teas are enhanced by longer or shorter infusion times.

HOW TO PREPARE AND DRINK A PROPER TEA - THE MAIN FACTORS

THE IMPORTANCE OF THE WATER,
WATER TEMPERATURE, INFUSION TIMES,
CHOICE OF ACCESSORIES, QUANTITY OF TEA,
OPTIMAL STORAGE METHOD FOR TEA

Among the secrets discovered in the various phases of working with tea leaves lies the promise of achieving the perfect cup of tea. However, purchasing high-quality tea is essential but not sufficient in itself to successfully savor a good cup of this beverage. Poor preparation can ruin a fine product or fail to bring out all the fragrances and aromas it has to offer.

Tea preparation may seem like a simple task, involving pouring hot water over dry leaves and waiting a few minutes. However, once the brew is in the cup, it might turn out too dark, sour, bitter, strong, or simply unpleasant to drink without adding sugar, milk, lemon, or honey to correct it. Instead of blaming the quality of the tea, you can experiment with a few simple tricks to achieve a better, and sometimes surprisingly excellent, result. Always keep your personal preferences and tastes in mind. Once you've selected a quality tea, don't hesitate to experiment with the process until you achieve a fully satisfying result. Below, we discuss the main factors that play a role in preparing a good cup of tea.

THE IMPORTANCE OF THE WATER

The quality of the water used for the infusion is just as crucial as the quality of the dried tea leaves. The color and aroma of the brew in your cup depend on the type of water used during preparation. By assessing the final result, it becomes evident that good water enhances the quality of the tea, while poor water can alter the infusion even when using the finest leaves.

Lu Yu, in *The Classic of Tea*, recommended using the same water that nourished the tea plant while it was growing. While this might not always be practical, you can opt for mineral or spring water. What's important is that the water is pure, odorless, colorless, mildly acidic (with a pH less than 7), soft (measured in French degrees; in this case, soft water does not exceed a limit of 8° F), and has a minimal mineral content (with a dry residue < 50 mg/l).

WATER TEMPERATURE

Using a water boiler with temperature control will enable you to achieve the best extraction possible from your favorite tea. It's essential to avoid letting the water boil, except for hygienic reasons. Boiling water loses its oxygen content, a critical factor in transferring aromatic compounds to a gaseous state, allowing them to be perceived as a scent. Moreover, after boiling, the minerals in the water tend to form a film on the surface, which doesn't interact well with tea.

Maintaining control over water temperature and other essential parameters helps prevent mistakes and maintains a good balance in the brew, considering factors like tannins, amino acids, minerals, and aromatic compounds. Excessively high temperatures can "burn" the tea, destroying amino acids and aromatic compounds, while also accelerating the extraction of polyphenols, resulting in a more bitter and sour taste. On the other hand, excessively low temperatures can prevent some teas from fully unfurling and achieving the right balance. Here are some general guidelines for water temperature:

- 160-185°F (70-85°C) for Japanese green teas and delicate, young, freshly picked teas.
- 175-185°F (80-85°C) for green, yellow, and white teas.
- 185-195°F (85-90°C) for red teas with buds and spring Darjeeling teas.
- 185-205°F (85-95°C) for Wulong or rolled teas.
- 195-210°F (90-98°C) for fermented, compressed, black Indian, or Singhalese teas.

THE ART OF TEA MAKING

INFUSION TIMES

This parameter can be highly debated, and it often depends on personal preferences for a more delicate or intense taste. Generally, high-quality teas require shorter infusion times compared to standard quality teas. Freshness also plays a crucial role: young and fresh spring teas or teas with a high percentage of buds require even shorter infusion times.

CHOICE OF ACCESSORIES

There's no definitive answer about the choice of teapot, and it can't be said that one preparation method, whether Eastern or Western, is superior to the other. However, it's accurate to say that certain teas and specific accessories can lead to optimal results, highlighting the tea's quality. Some teas, like fermented or Wulong, fully express their potential with the Gong Fu Cha method, and their quality can often be gauged by the number of possible infusions. On the other hand, certain teas benefit from longer infusion times to release their aromas, making the Western method more suitable.

QUANTITY OF TEA

As previously discussed, there is no absolute rule when it comes to tea preparation. Instead, two distinct approaches exist: Eastern and Western. The first favors short infusion times and a larger quantity of tea leaves, while the second opts for a smaller quantity of tea in a single infusion over an extended period.

In the Eastern method, the amount of dried leaves is tailored to fit a very small container like the Yi Xing teapot or Gaiwan teacup. When employing the Gong Fu Cha method, the ratio of leaves should be approximately one-third to half the size of the container. For a vessel with a capacity of 2/3 of a cup (150 ml), you'll need around 1/8 oz (5-6 grams) of tea.

Conversely, in the Western approach with a container of the same size, the quantity is nearly halved. The tea-to-water ratio typically ranges from 1/5 to 1/7, requiring an estimate of about 1/16 oz (2-3 g) for every 2/3 of a cup (150 ml).

THE ART OF TEA MAKING

THE ART OF TEA MAKING 茶

Choosing the right accessories enhances the tea's flavour, colour and scent.

THE ART OF TEA MAKING

OPTIMAL STORAGE METHOD FOR TEA

Tea's adversaries are light, moisture, and odors. To preserve the freshness and aroma of high-quality tea, it's essential to adhere to a few straightforward storage guidelines. First and foremost, avoid storing tea in a glass or transparent container, and be cautious when purchasing from anyone who stores it this way. Storing quality tea improperly can cause it to lose its sensory properties. Always opt for containers that are both airtight and opaque.

Tea leaves possess high porosity and can readily absorb moisture and odors from their surroundings. Tea containers should be situated in cool, well-ventilated areas, far removed from strong-smelling items such as spices, coffee, cheese, or other aromatic foods.

Grand cru teas should ideally be consumed within one year from the time of harvesting.

THE ART OF TEA MAKING

THE ART OF TEA MAKING

39

THE RUSSIAN ART OF TEA MAKING: THE SAMOVAR

The samovar and its usage represent quintessential and captivating facets of Russian culture. Since the nineteenth century, when the tradition of tea permeated every corner of Russian life, the samovar has held the esteemed position of the heart of every household and a symbol of hospitality.

This unique apparatus, with its distinctive form and purpose, functions as a self-boiling kettle, ensuring that water is consistently maintained at the ideal temperature. While in the past, the water was heated over an open brazier, contemporary samovars are typically electric and crafted from materials such as steel, silver, gold, or porcelain. Positioned atop the hot water boiler is a recess where the teapot is nestled.

- Russian tea is prepared using a highly concentrated, robust dark tea, often in a ratio of equal parts water and tea leaves.
- Following filtration, the teapot is positioned on the samovar, where the concentrated tea remains warm, thanks to the water vapor emitted by the boiler.
- When someone desires a cup of tea, approximately 0.4-0.8 inches (1-2 cm) of concentrated tea is poured into a cup, then diluted by adding hot water from the samovar's spigot.
- This tea is typically served with accompaniments such as jam, blinis, milk, orange peel, candied fruit, and sugar cubes. The sugar cubes are traditionally clamped between the teeth to sweeten the tea as it travels from the cup to the mouth.

THE MOROCCAN ART OF TEA MAKING: MINT TEA

Mint and wormwood infusions hold a cherished place in North African traditions, where tea consumption was introduced relatively late in the mid-nineteenth century by the British. During this period, the Crimean War posed a threat to British trade routes with Slavic nations, prompting the English to explore new markets in North Africa. Tea quickly captivated the Moroccan population, and local customs led to the incorporation of traditional flavors like mint, wormwood, and sage into the new beverage.

Green tea infused with mint has evolved into a daily ritual, observed during important business negotiations, significant family moments, or simply to extend a warm welcome to a guest. The Chinese Gunpowder green tea, originating from Zhejiang, serves as the preferred variety in Morocco and other Arab countries for their tea ceremonies.

To prepare mint tea, begin by bringing water to a boil.

- Place two tablespoons of Gunpowder green tea in a silver or metal teapot, then pour some boiling water over the tea leaves. Give it a quick rinse and discard the water.
- Next, add a handful of fresh Nana mint leaves and 5 to 7 cubes of white sugar.
- Stir and allow it to infuse for 4-5 minutes.
- Pour the tea into a glass and then transfer it back into the pot.
- Repeat this process three times to thoroughly blend all the ingredients.
- Place a teaspoon of pine nuts into the empty glass.
- Mint tea is traditionally served with pine nuts and typical Arab desserts crafted with honey, coconut, walnuts, almonds, and sesame seeds.

ICED TEA: PREPARATION METHODS

When you have high-quality tea, preparing a delicious iced tea to share with friends at a party, enjoy as an original aperitif, or simply quench your thirst on hot summer days is remarkably straightforward.

There are two methods for preparation: one involving heat and the other staying cold.

The hot infusion results in a stronger, more robustly flavored beverage. To prepare it, use approximately 1/16 oz (2-3 g) of tea for every 2/3 cup (150 ml) of water. Extend the infusion time by one minute beyond what's indicated in the preparation tables. After filtering, pour the tea into a shaker filled with ice cubes. If desired, add a tablespoon of liquid brown sugar to sweeten. Serve the tea in red wine glasses, garnished with fresh fruit.

The cold infusion produces a delicate, crystal-clear beverage, almost akin to scented water, with no lingering bitterness. Given the time, this method is certainly the superior choice. Follow these steps:

- Place about 1/2 oz (15-18 g) of tea in a glass jar.
- Pour a liter of cool or tepid water over the tea leaves.
- Immediately refrigerate the jar, allowing approximately 4 hours for green tea and around 6 hours for Wulong, black, or blended tea to infuse. It's advisable not to prepare the infusion at room temperature, as the dry leaves might contain spore-forming bacteria. These spores remain inactive at hot or cold temperatures but may reactivate at room temperature in the presence of water.
- Before serving, strain the iced tea into large wine glasses and garnish with fresh fruit.

THE ART OF TEA MAKING

PROFESSIONAL TEA TASTING
EQUIPMENT AND ASSESSMENT METHODS

The first comparative tea tastings and competitions were held in China as early as the 8th century AD. In the West, professional tasting gained prominence in the late 1800s when imported tea from China and India was often adulterated. New and old harvests were blended together, or tea leaves were mixed with those of other plants. This necessitated quality checks on imported products before they could be sold. Tea companies started training professional tea tasters and tea blenders.

Professional tea tasting allows for the sampling and comparison of numerous teas, establishing a universal standard of assessment based on specific parameters. The professional tea tasting set is made of white porcelain and includes three pieces: a bowl-shaped cup, a small cup with a notched edge and a handle, and a lid. This set enables the preparation of small quantities of various teas while maintaining a consistent leaf-to-water ratio. The goal of professional tasting is to compare various samples of the same tea from different tea gardens and describe the quality and flaws of each. Successful tasting requires a deep understanding of the general characteristics of the tea under analysis. Comparative tests reveal differences and similarities, aiding in the selection of the highest quality teas.

Regardless of the location, tea tasting adheres to the same ISO standards and employs identical equipment. While ISO standards aren't legal regulations, they specify rules for cups (with precise instructions on weight, diameter, curvature, height, shape, lid, etc.), the quantity of tea, infusion time, and water temperature that must be followed. Effective comparative analysis of different teas can only occur if all these parameters are maintained, with the only variable being the type of tea being analyzed.

Professional tea tasting is based on cups that are a natural evolution of the Gaiwan cup used in China. The method involves:

1. Placing the dry tea leaves to be assessed on a saucer.
2. Setting up the tasting set, which includes a bowl, notched cup, and lid.
3. Adding approximately 1/16 oz (2.8 g) of tea to the bottom of the notched cup.
4. Pouring about 2/3 cup (140 ml) of water heated to 208°F (98°C) over the leaves, covering the cup with the lid, and letting it infuse for 6 minutes.
5. After infusion, keeping the lid securely on the notched cup and filtering all the tea into the bowl.
6. Beginning the tasting, which involves analyzing the dry leaves, the liquor (the actual tea), and the soaked leaves.

WHEN IT COMES TO THE DRY AND SOAKED LEAVES, THE TASTER WILL PERFORM THE FOLLOWING:
- A visual analysis, which includes evaluating the shape and size of the leaves, their color and brilliance, composition (e.g., shoots only, shoots with open leaves, leaves only, etc.), and identifying any flaws and imperfections (e.g., broken leaves, stains, fungi, twigs, etc.).
- An olfactory analysis, focusing on aromatic notes.
- A tactile analysis, considering the consistency, friability, elasticity, and softness of the leaves.

CONCERNING THE LIQUOR, THE TASTER WILL PERFORM THE FOLLOWING:
- A visual analysis, assessing the color and clearness of the tea.
- An olfactory analysis, evaluating the scent of the tea in terms of intensity and persistence.
- A taste analysis, taking into account aromatic persistence, tactile sensations in the mouth, taste, and the combination of flavor and aroma.

It's important to note that sensitivity to odors is subjective and varies from one individual to another. Recognizing odors is a matter of practice, involving associating the sensations perceived with information and experiences stored in one's memory. Scents play a crucial role in successful tea tasting, and practice in this area allows for effective assessment of tea quality, based on achieving the right balance between aromatic notes.

In terms of taste analysis, particular importance is attributed to the following:
Body or texture: which is determined by the tea's astringency, softness, smoothness, temperature, heat, freshness, etc. These tactile experiences are felt in the mouth, on the tongue, lips, and palate.
Taste: which encompasses the flavor (sweet, salty, bitter, sour, umami) and texture of the tea.
Scent: detected by the nose through direct olfactory input or inhalation; a pleasant smell is referred to as perfume, while an unpleasant one is labeled as a smell.
Aroma a combination of taste and scent, detected by the mouth through indirect olfactory input. This phase is considered the most important in tea tasting.

TEA SCENTS

"Pure" original teas possess specific scents attributed to the cultivar type, climate conditions, soil chemical composition, and processing methods developed over the years. Continuous research helps us understand the specific characteristics and typical notes of each tea.

There are macro olfactory families corresponding to the scents detected while tasting tea.

These families are not mutually exclusive, and their notes can blend harmoniously:

VEGETABLE FAMILY: Includes scents like freshly cut grass, hay, herbs, cooked vegetables (asparagus, artichokes, spinach, zucchini), moss, mushrooms, humus, and undergrowth.

FRUITY FAMILY: Encompasses aromas of apples, pears, grapes, plums, peaches, apricots, tropical fruits, citrus fruits, cooked fruits (black cherry jam, plum jam), and nuts (dates, walnuts, almonds, hazelnuts, chestnuts).

FLORAL FAMILY: Comprises scents of jasmine, orchid, rose, orange blossom, peony, osmanthus, hawthorn, linden, and wildflowers.

AQUATIC FAMILY: Includes seaweed, crustaceans, fish skin, and mollusks.

WOODY FAMILY: Encompasses green wood, dry wood, cedar, cigar, bark, and sandalwood.

"CONFISERIE" FAMILY: Consists of aromas like honey, butter, cream, milk, sugar, vanilla, chocolate, and caramel.

BALSAMIC FAMILY: Comprises pine, resin, and incense scents.

SPICY FAMILY: Includes aromas of cinnamon, pepper, nutmeg, and cloves.

EMPYREUMATIC FAMILY: Encompasses scents of tobacco, cocoa, smoked, toasted, and grilled.

ANIMAL FAMILY: Includes aromas of game, fur, cat urine, wet dog, and leather.

In this section, we will provide a brief and concise glossary of terms used to taste and assess the quality of tea. This list is not exhaustive or technically comprehensive because different cultures have developed distinct lexicons, and each tea taster and expert may contribute their own unique terminology. The overview is meant to serve as a general introduction, offering some of the colorful and diverse expressions associated with the world of tea.

COMMENTS ON THE APPEARANCE OF LEAVES

Body: Relates to the appearance of the leaves, which can be old or tender, light or heavy, and have thick or thin flesh. Generally, tender, thick, and heavy leaves are considered the best.

Clear tip: The white down on the shoot is known as the "white tip." If the shoot has several tips covered in thick down, these are defined as "clear tips," and the tips can be gold, silver, or grey.

Dry: Dry tea leaves that have not yet been steeped.

Flawed leaf: A badly cut leaf presenting rough edges on both sides of the cut.

Heaviness: Rolled leaves that feel substantial in the hand.

Infusion: Steeped tea leaves removed from the water.

Powder: The residue produced after rolling, generally associated with low-quality tea, often used in tea bags.

Shoots: Tender tips, covered with white down, that have not grown into a full leaf.

Tender leaves: Tea consisting mainly of shoots with one or two leaves; these are round, narrow, thin, and have sharp pointy tips.

Uneven leaves: Leaves of irregular shape or thickness.

Well proportioned leaves: Leaves with a uniform shape, whether big or small, long or short, heavy or light.

COMMENTS ON THE COLOR OF LEAVES

Black-brown: Brownish black, with shades of grey.

Brilliant: A leaf of bright, vivid color.

Even: A bright, homogeneous color.

Grass green: Pale green, indicating old or low-quality leaves, or that the enzyme activity has not been successfully blocked.

Green-black: Well-proportioned, velvety, and even green, with shades of black.

Rich green: Shiny jade green.

Matte: The typical color of old, lusterless leaves.

Mixed: Leaves of uneven color.

Rust: Dark, matte red.

COMMENTS ON THE SCENT

Aroma: The overall scent perceived indirectly in the mouth.

Bouquet: The set of fragrances perceived in the nose.

Burnt: The smell of burning caused by blocked enzyme activity or inappropriate heating or drying.

Delicate aroma: An elegant aroma in which no blend is perceived.

Elegant aroma: A graceful and elegant floral aroma in which no one particular flower can be detected.

Grass aroma: The scent of grass and leaves.

Pure and semi-sweet: A pure, balanced aroma.

Sweet aroma: An aroma similar to honey or syrup, reminiscent of lychees.

Toasted rice aroma: Similar to the smell of popcorn, typical of lightly toasted teas.

Vegetable aroma: Similar to the smell of freshly boiled cabbage; this term is often used to describe green tea.

PROFESSIONAL TEA TASTING

COMMENTS ON THE COLOR OF THE LIQUOR

Brilliant: Clear, shiny liquid.

Brilliant green: Rich green with shades of yellow; clear and bright, this is the color of top-quality green tea.

Cloudy: Unclear liquor with suspended substances.

Golden: Mainly yellow with shades of orange; light and brilliant, just like gold.

Green-yellow: Green with a hint of yellow.

Light yellow: Yellow and clear.

Liquor: In technical jargon, this is the liquid you drink, namely the tea itself.

Orange: Yellow with a hint of red, just like the color of ripe oranges.

Orange-red: Dark yellow with shades of red.

Red: Overheated or old liquor, light or dark red in color.

Yellow-green: Yellow with a hint of green.

COMMENTS ON THE TASTE OF THE LIQUOR

Astringent: Dries the mouth due to non-oxidized polyphenols (typical of green tea) reacting with the proteins in the saliva.

Bitter: An intense, bitter, and sour aroma that dulls the taste buds slightly.

Brisk: A strong, invigorating, and refreshing flavor.

Crude and sour: An unripe, strong, sour flavor, usually due to insufficient withering.

Crude and tasteless: Insipid, tending toward bitter.

Fresh: Fresh and delicious, used to indicate slightly acidic tea that leaves a feeling of freshness in the mouth.

Full-bodied: A strong, full-flavored infusion.

Generous: Ripe and dense; rich in flavor, without being cloyingly sweet.

Grassy and sour: A strong, sour grassy taste.

Malty: A flavor reminiscent of malt; this is an indication of good quality tea.

Metallic: The unpleasant taste typical of badly withered tea.

Persistent: Leaves a lingering flavor in the mouth.

Pungent: Astringent without being bitter.

Pure and delicate: Ripe but not too dense.

Refined: A subtle, sophisticated taste and aroma.

Rounded: Fills the mouth with a feeling of fullness.

Semi-sweet: Sweet but balanced aroma.

Smoked: Tea dried on smoky flames, providing a smoky aroma.

Strong: A full, highly astringent taste, typical of a dark liquor.

Subtle: A flavor marked by delicate yet complex aromas.

Sweet: Slightly sugary, not astringent.

Tannic: The flavor of liquors rich in tannins, or polyphenols.

Tasteless or flat: The thin, bodiless taste of humid tea.

Umami: One of the five basic flavors perceived by the taste buds (the others are "sweet," "salty," "bitter," and "sour"); it is mostly used in Asian cuisine to describe the taste of glutamates, which can be detected in certain Japanese green teas.

Velvety: A harmonious flavor reminiscent of the softness of silk and velvet.

Watery: Thin tea due to insufficient or inadequate infusion.

GREEN TEA - CHINA

This is the most popular tea in the East. China is the world's largest producer of green tea and can undoubtedly claim to offer the greatest variety. Green tea accounts for approximately 75% of the tea produced in China. The remaining 25% is mainly divided among other tea "colors," including red, fermented black, and Wulong. White and yellow teas are considered "niche" products, making up only a small percentage of production.

World-renowned Chinese green teas are traditionally grown in Anhui, Zhejiang, and Fujian. The Anhui region produces highly esteemed teas such as Lu Mu Dan, Huang Shan Mao Feng, Huo Shan Huang Ya, Liu An Gua Pian, and Tai Ping Hou Kui, to name just a few. The Zhejiang region, known for the precious Long Jing, also mass-produces Gunpowder, a tea that is often of mediocre quality and exported worldwide. The area around Fuzhou, in the Fujian region, boasts the highest production of Jasmine green tea.

Other excellent products come from the Yunnan mountains and from the province of Jiangsu, where Bi Luo Chun is second only to the famous Long Jing.

Green tea is the only category of teas whose leaves are not processed in a way that alters their chemical properties, thus preserving more than 85% of their polyphenol content and their natural green color.

The freshly picked leaves are spread on bamboo racks and left to dry. Subsequently, depending on the chosen method, they are subjected to dry heat (in special concave containers similar to woks), air, or steam. The high temperature reached during this process blocks enzyme activity and prevents the natural oxidation process, allowing the tea leaves to maintain their green color. This step is crucial in producing quality green tea and releases the sweet floral, chestnut, and walnut fragrance characteristic of green teas.

The subsequent steps vary widely depending on the desired product. The leaves can be rolled to give them various forms: twisted into spirals, folded, crushed, or tightly rolled into small pearls.

The final drying phase further reduces the residual moisture content in the leaves. The green tea is now ready to be packaged and distributed to the market.

HOW TO PREPARE CHINESE GREEN TEA

Green tea doesn't require the leaves to be briefly rinsed, which is why the infusion can be prepared directly in a tall and narrow glass cup, allowing you to appreciate the slow movement of the leaves as they seem to dance, suspended in the water. However, according to experts, the Gaiwan teacup is the best method for preparing more refined and delicate teas. It consists of three parts: the cup, lid, and saucer. The lid is used to hold the leaves, whether it's being used as a cup or a teapot for multiple infusions. It can be made from different materials, but for green teas, glass or porcelain is recommended.

GREEN TEA

HOW TO USE A GAIWAN TEACUP

When using a Gaiwan cup as a teapot, it's recommended to follow these steps:

1. Place the Gaiwan cup, teapot, and glasses on the ceremonial table.
2. After bringing the water to the desired temperature, pour the hot water into the Gaiwan to heat and rinse it.
3. Discard the water and add the desired quantity of tea leaves into the Gaiwan (around 1/4 or 1/3 the volume of the Gaiwan).
4. Pour the water into the Gaiwan, and once it's filled, place the lid on it and wait.
5. Pour the tea directly into the cups or stop the infusion by pouring the brew into the teapot.

During this step, you can use a strainer to prevent the leaves from being poured into the cups. With the Gaiwan teacup, the infusion can be repeated several times, varying the time from 20 to 40 seconds according to personal taste. Between preparations, it's interesting to smell the inner portion of the lid to observe how the aromas are released and develop over multiple infusions.

A BIT OF ETIQUETTE FOR TEA DRINKING IF YOU GO TO CHINA

In China, when tea is served to you, it's good manners to bring the index and middle fingers of your right hand together, slightly bend them, and tap the table twice, symbolizing a small bow. This small ceremony is performed to show appreciation and gratitude toward the host and dates back to the Qing dynasty when Emperor Qianlong was in power.

During one of his journeys to the south, the Emperor disguised himself as a servant. When he reached a tea house, the owner, thinking he was a servant, gave him a teapot and ordered him to serve tea to the eunuch who had accompanied him on his journey. The eunuch, unable to bow to his lord due to the need to maintain his disguise, put his two fingers together to form a bow out of respect. Over time, this gesture of thanks spread among the common people until it became a pleasant courtesy exchanged among friends.

GREEN TEA

ANJI BAI CHA

TYPE: GREEN TEA

AREA OF PROVENANCE: CHINA, ZHEJIANG, ANJI

Anji Bai Cha tea derives its name from the village of Anji situated in the Mu Tian mountain ranges, where the plantations for this exceptional green tea flourish. The pristine environment, characterized by bamboo forests, clouds, rain, and fertile soil, makes this location ideal for cultivating this unique tea.

In Chinese, "Bai" means white, which is why it is sometimes referred to as Anji White Tea, despite being classified as a green tea. The term "white" is derived from the shoots of the tea plant, which are of this color before undergoing processing. An ancient Chinese book mentions a tea plant with pale white leaves resembling jade. This account was regarded as a legend until the 1980s when a tea plant with white shoots was discovered near Anji. Experts believe this is the same plant mentioned in the ancient book, and Anji Bai Cha is produced from the leaves of this particular botanical specimen. The leaves are harvested in early spring, before rising temperatures cause them to turn green.

This tea is rich in amino acids, containing nearly twice the amount found in other green teas, and it possesses calming and stress-reducing properties.

TASTING NOTES

Dry: The shoots are hand-worked to form flat, thin blades.

Liquor: It has a pale yellow, crystal-clear appearance, with a pleasantly delicate taste that lingers and refreshes, accompanied by a subtle hint of orchid.

Infusion: The young shoots are light green, tending toward white. The harvesting method involves one shoot and one leaf.

PREPARATION

Western method: Use approximately 1/16 oz (2-3 grams) for every 2/3 cup (150 ml) of water at 175°F (80°C) for 2 minutes.

Eastern method: Use 1/8 oz (5 grams) for every 2/3 cup (150 milliliters) of water at 175°F (80°C) for up to 3 infusions, each lasting 20-30 seconds.

Recommended with: Anji Bai Cha pairs well with lightly salted foods, white meats, vegetables, and fish.

GREEN TEA

JADE COLUMN - YU ZHU

TYPE: GREEN TEA
AREA OF PROVENANCE: CHINA, YUNNAN, PU'ER

This tea hails from the plantations in the Pu'er region of Yunnan and boasts a unique appearance that inspired its name. It comprises a single shoot that is meticulously processed to resemble a jade-colored column.

It is truly exceptional, much like all the green teas from the Yunnan mountains, and is crafted by carefully selecting the finest shoots from the spring harvest. When brewed, it encapsulates the rich culture and art of Yunnan tea, making it a poetic and special choice for grand occasions.

TASTING NOTES

Dry: A single, rolled, light green shoot with hints of silver.
Liquor: In the cup, it displays a clear ivory color. The taste is soft, lingering, and exudes a delicate floral aroma with underlying notes of dried fruit (walnut) and fresh fruit (peach).
Infusion: The leaves unfurl into perfectly intact and consistently yellow-green leaves.

PREPARATION

Eastern method: Use 1/8 oz (5 grams) for every 2/3 cup (150 milliliters) of water at 175°F (80°C) for 3-5 infusions, each lasting 20-30 seconds.

Recommended with: This tea pairs excellently with lightly salted foods, rice, vegetables, poultry, and pork.

GREEN TEA

DONG TING BI LUO CHUN

TYPE: GREEN TEA

AREA OF PROVENANCE: CHINA, JIANGSU, DONG TING

This ancient Chinese tea, second in fame only to the Xi Hu Long Jing, originates from the Temple of Ling Yuan Bi Luo Peak in Shandong. It was originally named Xia Si Xiang Ren, meaning "amazing fragrance." However, Emperor Qing bestowed upon it the name Bi Luo Chun and elevated its status to Imperial tea.

Dong Ting Bi Luo Chun, crafted in its region of origin, is meticulously processed by hand, and only the tender shoots and first leaves are carefully harvested. To give you an idea of its delicacy, it takes approximately 120,000 leaves to produce just one kilogram of Bi Luo Chun First Grade.

TASTING NOTES

Dry: The light green, tender leaves are slightly curled, and the shoots are adorned with a silvery down.
Liquor: The tea yields a brilliant yellow liquor, boasting a highly refreshing character characterized by soft floral notes.
Infusion: Steeping the leaves results in a brilliant green hue, with lingering floral notes that intermingle with hints of nuts, particularly chestnuts.

PREPARATION

Western method: Use approximately 1/16 oz (2-3 grams) of tea for every 2/3 cup (150 milliliters) of water at 165-175°F (75-80°C), and steep for 2-3 minutes.
Eastern method: Employ 1/8 oz (5 grams) of tea for every 2/3 cup (150 milliliters) of water at 165-175°F (75-80°C), allowing for up to 3-4 infusions, each lasting 20-40 seconds.

Recommended with: Dong Ting Bi Luo Chun complements a variety of dishes, including rice, fish, poultry, pork, vegetables, and spicy foods.

HUANG SHAN MAO FENG

TYPE: GREEN TEA

AREA OF PROVENANCE: CHINA, ANHUI, SHE XIAN, HUANG SHAN MOUNTAINS

A timeless Chinese adage proclaims that teas from the mountains are the finest, and among China's most renowned mountain ranges for Grand Cru teas, the Huang Shan Mountains are the most famous. In this category, Huang Shan Mao Feng stands tall as one of the ten most beloved green teas. When poured into a cup, the tea presents a light and brilliant liquor, while its taste offers an intense and revitalizing aroma, leaving behind a sweet aftertaste.

TASTING NOTES

Dry: Comprising tender shoots adorned with delicate white down and slightly curved leaves near the buds, the tea's appearance is reminiscent of orchid buds.

Liquor: The tea yields a brilliant, clear gold-colored liquor. Its aroma is intense and captivating, featuring a sweet, lingering aftertaste. There's a harmonious balance between the floral notes (orchid, magnolia), ripe fruits (apricot, mango), and chestnut undertones.

Infusion: Steeping the young green-yellow shoots releases their tender essence, with hints of nuttiness.

PREPARATION

Western method: Utilize approximately 1/16 oz (2-3 grams) of tea for every 2/3 cup (150 milliliters) of water at 175°F (80°C), steeping for 3 minutes.

Eastern method: Employ 1/8 oz (5 grams) of tea for every 2/3 cup (150 milliliters) of water at 175°F (80°C), allowing for 3-5 infusions, each lasting 20-30 seconds.

Recommended with: Huang Shan Mao Feng pairs well with lightly salted dishes, spicy foods, flavored cheeses, grilled fish, fruits, and hazelnut pie.

GREEN TEA 茶

HUO SHAN HUANG YA

TYPE: GREEN TEA

AREA OF PROVENANCE: CHINA, ANHUI, HUO SHAN

While often marketed in the West as a rare yellow tea, Huo Shan Huang Ya is, in fact, a green tea cultivated in the Huo Shan mountains of Anhui. During the fermentation process, the enzymes responsible for oxidation are blocked, resulting in the young shoots taking on a yellow hue. This process is the origin of the name "Huang Ya," which means "yellow shoot." Due to its refined characteristics, Huo Shan Huang Ya was offered as a tribute to the Imperial court during the Ming and Qing dynasties.

TASTING NOTES

Dry: The tea features brilliant green leaves that are narrow and elongated, resembling a bird's tongue. The outer surface of the leaves is adorned with a light down.

Liquor: The liquor is golden yellow with an aroma reminiscent of nuts, such as chestnuts and hazelnuts, followed by a sweet aftertaste.

Infusion: Steeping the leaves reveals a light green to yellow hue with highly intense floral notes.

PREPARATION

Western method: Use approximately 1/16 oz (2-3 grams) of tea for every 2/3 cup (150 milliliters) of water at 175°F (80°C), steeping for 2-3 minutes.

Eastern method: Employ 1/8 oz (5 grams) of tea for every 2/3 cup (150 milliliters) of water at 175°F (80°C), allowing for 4-5 infusions, each lasting 20-30 seconds.

Recommended with: Huo Shan Huang Ya pairs well with rice, vegetables, shellfish, chicken curry, cakes, and hazelnut biscuits.

 GREEN TEA

LIU AN GUA PIAN

TYPE: GREEN TEA

AREA OF PROVENANCE: CHINA, ANHUI, JINZHAI

Originally known as Gua Zi Pian, meaning "sunflower seed" due to its shape resembling the popular Chinese snack, this tea eventually adopted the simpler name Gua Pian. Liu An, on the other hand, refers to the village of its origin. Regarded as a superior quality tea, it was presented as a tribute to the Imperial Court during the Ming dynasty. Only the small leaves are processed, following the removal of the shoots.

TASTING NOTES

Dry: The tea boasts elongated, narrow emerald green leaves.

Liquor: The liquor is golden yellow with an intense sweet taste, accompanied by flowery, fruity, and mildly empyreumatic (smoky) notes. The taste lingers persistently in the mouth and has excellent thirst-quenching properties, making it ideal for hot summer days.

Infusion: Steeping the leaves reveals large, regularly shaped, brilliant green leaves.

PREPARATION

Western method: Use approximately 1/16 oz (2-3 grams) of tea for every 2/3 cup (150 milliliters) of water at 175°F (80°C), steeping for 2 minutes.

Eastern method: Employ 1/8 oz (5 grams) of tea for every 2/3 cup (150 milliliters) of water at 175°F (80°C), allowing for 3-4 infusions, each lasting 20-30 seconds.

Recommended with: Gua Pian pairs well with lightly salted foods, Parma ham and melon, mixed salads, and fruit salad.

JASMINE PEARL - JASMINE LONG ZHU

TYPE: SCENTED GREEN TEA

AREA OF PROVENANCE: CHINA, FUJIAN

This Fujian green tea is hand-rolled into pearls, each consisting of one tender shoot and two leaves, creating a classic tea with a delightful sweet taste and a delicate jasmine aroma. The natural scent is derived from contact with fresh jasmine flowers. The production of this tea occurs in two distinct phases: during the spring, the leaves are processed using the same technique as for green tea, and in the summer, when jasmine is in full bloom, it is harvested and added to the previously processed tea leaves. This allows the tea leaves to absorb the fragrant jasmine perfume. The higher the frequency of contact between the leaves and flowers, the better the quality of the tea, albeit at a higher cost for the pearls. Experiencing this tea is an absolute delight.

TASTING NOTES

Dry: The tea appears as small, silvery pearls with an enchanting jasmine scent.

Liquor: The liquor has a dark, matte yellow color, with intense and lingering flowery notes that grace the mouth. It feels soft and slightly astringent.

Infusion: Steeping the rolled leaves and shoots reveals brilliant light green hues.

PREPARATION

Western method: Use approximately 1/16 oz (2-3 grams) of tea for every 2/3 cup (150 milliliters) of water at 185°F (85°C), steeping for 2-3 minutes.

Eastern method: Utilize approximately 1/8 oz (5-6 grams) of tea for every 2/3 cup (150 milliliters) of water at 185°F (85°C), allowing for 3-5 infusions, each lasting 20-40 seconds.

Recommended with: This tea pairs wonderfully with spicy foods, spiced white meats, shellfish, mozzarella, vegetables, potatoes, tarte tatin, or carrot cake.

LONG JING

ENGLISH TRANSLITERATION: LUNG CHING
TYPE: GREEN TEA
AREA OF PROVENANCE: CHINA, ZHEJIANG, XI HU

Long Jing tea, the most famous of all Chinese teas, boasts over a thousand years of history and was even mentioned in the first book dedicated to tea, "The Classic of Tea" by Lu Yu, dating back to the Tang dynasty.

The most original and highly prized Long Jing tea is Xi Hu Long Jing, which hails from the hillsides around Xi Hu and is protected by Chinese law as a food product. To attain PGI status (equivalent to the Italian DOCG for wines), the entire production process, from harvesting to packaging, must occur within the designated area of origin. This area measures 168 square kilometers, resulting in very limited quantities of this superb tea that barely meet domestic market demand. The best harvest of Xi Hu Long Jing, known as Shi Feng, is exceptionally rare to find outside China. However, good-quality Long Jing can be sampled more readily as its production has expanded to other provinces, making it the most widely grown green tea in China. It is characterized by an unmistakable aroma of boiled chestnuts.

TASTING NOTES

Dry: The tea leaves are narrow, flattened, and have an olive green-yellow color.

Liquor: The liquor appears as a brilliant golden yellow, with a soft taste featuring notes of boiled chestnuts, toasted nuts, and vanilla.

Infusion: The young shoots yield a brilliant green hue.

PREPARATION

Western method: Use approximately 1/16 oz (2-3 grams) of tea for every 2/3 cup (150 milliliters) of water at 175°F (80°C), steeping for 2-3 minutes.

Eastern method: Utilize approximately 1/8 oz (5-6 grams) of tea for every 2/3 cup (150 milliliters) of water at 175°F (80°C), allowing for 4-5 infusions, each lasting 20-40 seconds.

Recommended with: Long Jing tea pairs well with vegetable soups, lightly salted foods, rice, grilled fish, shellfish, flavored cheeses (such as Brie and Camembert), spiced white meats, and fruit.

GREEN LYCHEE

TYPE: SCENTED GREEN TEA
AREA OF PROVENANCE: CHINA, HUNAN

This green tea, scented with lychees, a native fruit of southern China and all of Southeast Asia, is hand-made and sold in the form of small balls. In this Hunan quality tea, the leaves are put into direct contact with fresh lychees. The flesh of this fruit is transparent and highly scented, and it was always enjoyed as a delicacy by the Imperial court. The tradition of scenting teas by direct contact with fruit and flowers originated in China, although nowadays artificial aromas are often added. This tea allows drinkers to experience the legacy of age-old knowledge born from patience and respect for natural products and processes.

The drink, with its enchanting, unmistakable taste and delicate but voluptuous scent, is a true delight: it is poetry in a cup and can be enjoyed either hot or cold, making it suitable for any season.

TASTING NOTES

Dry: The leaves are rolled into small balls of varying sizes, appearing as matte green with yellow streaks. They emit an intense scent of roses and grapes (moscato).

Liquor: The liquor is clear golden yellow, with the sweet hint of lychees and flowery notes from the tea leaves blending to form a unique aromatic bouquet. Floral notes of rose and gardenia merge with fruity notes of apricot, dried dates, and raisins.

Infusion: The dark matte green leaves open up completely, with the dominant scent being that of grapes (moscato).

PREPARATION

Western method: Use approximately 1/16 oz (2 grams) of tea for every 2/3 cup (150 milliliters) of water at 185°F (85°C), steeping for 2-3 minutes.

Eastern method: Employ 3-4 balls for every 2/3 cup (150 milliliters) of water at 185°F (85°C), allowing for 4-5 infusions, each lasting 20-40 seconds.

Recommended with: Lychee-scented green tea pairs well with yoghurt bavarois, Greek yoghurt and honey, vanilla desserts and custards, carrot and hazelnut cakes, white chocolate, Basmati rice, fresh fruit, and fruit salad with vodka.

TAI PING HOU KUI

TYPE: GREEN TEA

AREA OF PROVENANCE: CHINA, ANHUI, HUANG SHAN

Tai Ping Hou Kui is a unique green tea from Tai Ping (Anhui), situated at the foot of the Huang Shan mountains. Its exceptional appearance sets it apart from other green teas. During the processing of Tai Ping Hou Kui, the leaves are neither rolled nor compressed. This method results in its distinctive, unmistakable appearance: unusually long, flattened leaves that can reach up to 6 inches (15 centimeters) in length.

HOW TO PREPARE TAI PING HOU KUI

To prepare this extraordinary tea, which is unique not only for its refined aroma but also for its unusual appearance, it is not recommended to use a Gaiwan cup. The leaves of Tai Ping Hou Kui can grow up to 6 inches (15 cm) long, making it more suitable to use a tall glass or a tall glass teapot. Here's how to prepare it: Warm the glass cup or tall glass teapot by filling it with water heated to 175-185°F (80-85°C). Discard the water. Add approximately 1/16-1/8 oz (3-5 grams) of Tai Ping Hou Kui leaves. Pour in fresh, hot water brought up to the same temperature. If using a glass cup, you can drink the tea directly from it. If using a teapot, it's preferable to pour the brewed tea into a glass jar and then serve it in cups.

TASTING NOTES

Dry: The long, flat leaves are brilliant green.

Liquor: In the cup, it has a light, crystal-clear color. The taste is surprisingly delicate and sweet, reminiscent of orchids.

Infusion: The long, flat leaves lose their shine and become duller and lighter, with some red veins possibly appearing.

PREPARATION

Western method: Use approximately 1/16 oz (2-3 grams) of tea for every 2/3 cup (150 milliliters) of water at 175°F (80°C), steeping for 3 minutes.

Eastern method: Employ 1/8 oz (5 grams) of tea for every 2/3 cup (150 milliliters) of water at 175°F (80°C), allowing for 3 infusions, each lasting 30-40 seconds.

Recommended with: Tai Ping Hou Kui has delicate orchid notes and is best enjoyed on its own.

GREEN TEA

HOW TO PREPARE BLOOMING GREEN TEAS

To fully appreciate the display presented by blooming green tea blossoms, we recommend selecting a tall and slender glass cup or a lofty glass teapot, both measuring at least 6 inches (15 centimeters) in height.

Once you've poured water heated to approximately 175°F-185°F (80°C-85°C) over the tea "blossom," you'll need to patiently wait a few minutes to witness the mesmerizing Chinese art of skillfully binding tea buds unfold. These "tea blossoms" can be crafted exclusively from tea buds, as is the case with Lu Mu Dan, or they may be combined with various flowers such as jasmine, calendulas, amaranths, lilies, globe amaranths, or hibiscus. In addition to enhancing the infusion with a delicate floral aroma, these flowers offer a visually stunning and impressive spectacle that is certain to delight.

Lu Mu Dan, which resembles the shape of a chrysanthemum or a small rose, can also be prepared using a glass Gaiwan cup.

GREEN TEA

The slow and delicate unfurling of "blooming teas"

 GREEN TEA

LU MU DAN

TYPE: GREEN SCENTED TEA

AREA OF PROVENANCE: CHINA, ANHUI, SHE XIAN

This flower-shaped tea is meticulously crafted from green tea shoots harvested from the plantations on the Huang Shan mountains in the Anhui region, specifically from the area of She Xian. It can be considered a precursor to "blooming teas," which are intricate Chinese creations made by tying tea shoots together to form small spheres, towers, and even seated Buddhas.

Unlike many blooming teas, where the beauty of the budding flowers can be overshadowed by the mediocre quality of the tea leaves, Lu Mu Dan stands out. It is a rare blend of poetry and aesthetics, offering truly surprising aromatic notes. After steeping for a few minutes, this delicate rose-shaped tea unfurls to produce a clear and brilliant liquor with a sweet, honeyed flavor.

TASTING NOTES

Dry: Approximately a hundred small shoots are skillfully tied together to create a star-shaped bouquet.
Liquor: Brilliant, light in color, and crystal clear; the sweet taste is almost never astringent, with delicate but lingering notes of honey, licorice, and boiled chestnuts, which are typical of the finest Chinese green teas.
Infusion: Once steeped, the shoots in the star-shaped bouquet unfurl, resembling the shape of a chrysanthemum, carnation, or small rose.

PREPARATION

Use one bouquet for every 1 1/4 cups (30 centiliters) of water at 175°F-185°F (80°C-85°C) for a 2-3 minute infusion.

Recommended with: Lu Mu Dan pairs wonderfully with lightly salted foods, white meats, vegetables, fish, rice, and fruit.

GREEN TEA

Japanese cast iron teapots keep the water hot for longer.
For this reason, they were traditionally used as kettles.

GREEN TEA - JAPAN

Tea in all its forms is so widespread in Japanese society that it is a part of nearly every aspect of daily life. It is served with meals in restaurants (Bancha, Houjicha), prepared among friends or in small groups for refined social gatherings (Sencha, Gyokuro), and, of course, it symbolizes Zen philosophy during the tea ceremony (Matcha).

The annual production of green tea is not sufficient to meet domestic demand. A significant proportion of green tea sold in Japan is not actually produced locally; instead, it is cultivated and processed in China, Vietnam, or Indonesia using traditional methods.

In Japan, tea is harvested two to four times a year, with the spring crop being undoubtedly the best and most sought after. Japanese green tea is traditionally grown in the prefecture of Shizuoka, renowned for the finest Sencha, the prefecture of Kyoto, known for prestigious Matcha and Gyokuro, and the prefectures of Kagoshima and Kyushu in the southern part of the country.

In the past, this tea was entirely processed by hand (temomi-cha) through the skilled work of Temomi Masters who passed down their tradition from one generation to the next as a precious treasure to be preserved. Unfortunately, machinery has taken over in recent decades. However, a national competition is held every year to find the best temomi-cha or handmade tea. The first thirty winners fetch no less than 90,718 yen per pound (200,000 yen per kilogram).

In Japan, green tea retains its bright green color through a steaming method developed in Kyoto in 1738 by Nagatani Soen.

During this very brief heating phase, the high temperature reached blocks the enzymes responsible for oxidation and allows the tea to maintain its original color. This procedure also makes the leaves elastic and supple, making them easier to roll up.

Rolling takes about four hours and is performed on a heated surface called hoiro until the leaves turn dark green and needle-shaped.

Traditionally, the plantations producing the finest teas in Japan are "shaded." In the 20-30 days leading up to harvest, the tea plants are covered with canvas sheets to reduce exposure to sunlight. This shading technique enhances the sweetness of the tea by decreasing its catechin content, thereby reducing the astringency and bitterness commonly associated with some green teas.

GREEN TEA

HOW TO PREPARE JAPANESE GREEN TEA

The infusion method for Japanese green teas strikes a balance between the quick and repeated Chinese method and the longer, single infusion approach used in the West.

For teas like Bancha, Houjicha, and Genmaicha, a single infusion is employed, similar to the Western method, but with a relatively shorter steeping time.

For higher-quality teas such as Sencha or Gyokuro, an infusion lasting around 2-2.5 minutes is repeated three times.

HOW TO USE THE KYUSU TEAPOT

The Kyusu teapot, a small teapot made from various materials such as porcelain or glass, is traditionally used for preparing Japanese green teas. It features a specialized grid filter inside and a convenient side handle. Typically, it has a small capacity, holding between 1/2 and 1 1/4 cups (100 and 300 ml) of water.

If you don't have a water boiler with temperature control, you can follow these steps using the Kyusu teapot and three cups:

1. Bring water to a boil.
2. Place the tea leaves inside the teapot.
3. Fill two cups with hot water, leaving the third cup empty.
4. Use the empty cup to pour hot water from one cup to another. With each pour, the water's temperature drops by approximately 50°F (10°C).
5. Once the water temperature reaches around 175°F (80°C) for Sencha or 140°-160°F (60°-70°C) for Gyokuro, pour the water from the two cups into the Kyusu teapot.
6. Pour the tea directly into the cups.
7. Repeat the infusion up to three times, slightly reducing the steeping time with each subsequent infusion.

GREEN TEA

BANCHA KAKEGAWA

TYPE: GREEN TEA

AREA OF PROVENANCE: JAPAN, SHIZUOKA, KAKEGAWA

Bancha tea enthusiasts will immediately recognize the exceptional quality of this first flush Bancha, which hails from the renowned plantations of Kakegawa in the western part of the Shizuoka prefecture. Even for those who may not typically enjoy this type of tea, a single sip is enough to realize that it stands apart from the common Bancha teas commonly found in the market. With its low tannin content, it pairs perfectly with meals at any time of the day.

TASTING NOTES

Dry: The tea features large, intensely vibrant green leaves with a fruity scent and a touch of sweetness.
Liquor: The liquor appears yellow-green and slightly cloudy. It offers a fresh and tender taste with delicate herbal notes reminiscent of spinach and subtle marine undertones.
Infusion: The steeped leaves take on an intense dark green color, resembling the leaves of cooked spinach.

PREPARATION

For every 2/3 cup (150 milliliters) of water at 175°F (80°C), use approximately 1/16 oz (2-3 grams) of tea leaves and steep for about 2 1/2 minutes.

Recommended with: Slightly salty foods, Raw and cooked fish, Shellfish, Vegetables Rice

GENMAICHA

TYPE: GREEN TEA

AREA OF PROVENANCE: JAPAN, SHIZUOKA, FUKUROI

This Genmaicha tea originates from the Fukuroi plantations in the coastal plain of southwestern Shizuoka. It is crafted by blending first flush Spring Bancha, which is the most esteemed Bancha tea, with toasted brown rice.

A legend surrounds the origins of this tea: in the 15th century, a samurai was sipping his tea while strategizing with his men. His servant, Genmai, accidentally spilled a few grains of rice into the tea, which angered the samurai to the point of beheading his servant. However, after tasting the tea, the samurai realized it had a delightful aroma and flavor due to the rice. Full of regret, he decided to continue drinking his tea with rice in honor of his departed servant and named it Genmaicha. Another, more plausible story suggests that people living far from tea plantations mixed tea with rice to extend their supplies. Regardless of its origins, Genmaicha is now one of Japan's most popular teas, known for its distinctive hazelnut taste and sometimes referred to as "popcorn tea." Its low tannin content makes it suitable for any time of day, including when served cold.

TASTING NOTES

Dry: Brilliant green tea leaves blended with toasted rice grains and puffed maize (popcorn). The floral notes harmonize with the smoky, toasted aromas.

Liquor: The liquor appears intense yellow-green, with toasted rice notes perfectly complementing the sweetness of springtime Bancha. It leaves a surprising, lingering hazelnut flavor.

Infusion: The leaves turn dark green, and the toasted rice takes on a deeper hue.

PREPARATION

For every 2/3 cup (150 milliliters) of water at 175-185°F (80-85°C), use approximately 1/16 oz (2-3 grams) of tea leaves and steep for about 2-2.5 minutes.

Recommended with: Soups, Rice dishes, Raw or cooked fish, Shellfish, Vegetables, Nut biscuits

GYOKURO

TYPE: GREEN TEA
AREA OF PROVENANCE: JAPAN, SHIZUOKA, OKABE

This is the most highly valued Japanese tea, cultivated near Okabe in the Shizuoka prefecture, renowned for Gyokuro production.

In the three weeks leading up to harvest, the tea plantation is entirely covered with special sheets to shade the tea plants. This technique enhances the caffeine and amino acid content while reducing the catechin levels in the leaves. As a result, Gyokuro has a much milder, less astringent, and bitter taste, distinguishing it from certain other green teas.

TASTING NOTES

Dry: Dark green, very thin needle-like leaves.
Liquor: Green-yellow in color, slightly cloudy, exceptionally smooth and not astringent. Dominated by marine (seafood) aromas with floral notes, it has an umami flavor.
Infusion: The leaves turn into an intensely brilliant dark green.

PREPARATION

For every 2/3 cup (150 milliliters) of water at 140-160°F (60-70°C), use approximately 1/16 oz (2-3 grams) of tea leaves and steep for about 2.5 minutes.

Recommended with: Shellfish, Raw and cooked fish, Vegetables, Fresh and soft cheeses

HOUJICHA

TYPE: GREEN TEA

AREA OF PROVENANCE: JAPAN, SHIZUOKA, FUKUROI

This special Japanese tea is a delicately toasted Bancha, with the finest Houjicha being crafted from leaves harvested in the autumn from the Fukuroi plantations located in the coastal plain to the southwest of Shizuoka.

Houjicha is a very gentle tea with minimal tannin content, making it suitable for consumption at any time of the day and appropriate for children. It pairs well with a wide variety of dishes.

TASTING NOTES

Dry: Long, large, intense hazelnut and amber-colored leaves that exude a sophisticated toasted and floral aroma, accompanied by woody and slightly fruity notes.

Liquor: Brilliant warm brown with hints of old gold. The tea offers an aromatic mouthfeel reminiscent of toasted hazelnuts, leaving a lingering malty aftertaste.

Infusion: Dark, nearly black khaki color with a scent dominated by fruity and woody notes, with a hint of spiciness.

PREPARATION

For every 2/3 cup (150 milliliters) of water at 175-185°F (80-85°C), use approximately 1/16 oz (2-3 grams) of tea leaves and steep for about 2-3 minutes.

Recommended with: Grilled fish, Mollusks, Pork, Vegetables, Rice, Hazelnut pies and biscuits

GREEN TEA

KUKICHA

TYPE: GREEN TEA

AREA OF PROVENANCE: JAPAN, SHIZOUKA, KAKEGAWA

Kukicha is typically a tea that primarily utilizes the least valued part of the plant, the stems.

However, in this unique case, Kukicha is the result of processing Sencha first flush tea leaves from the Kakegawa plantations in Shizuoka. The result is remarkably surprising due to its distinct flavor and freshness, offering an unexpected harmony for the senses. It serves as an excellent starting point for exploring Japanese green teas and helps overcome any preconceptions about their herbal flavors being an acquired taste.

TASTING NOTES

Dry: A lovely assortment of light green stems that emit a fresh, clean scent with delicate, harmonious floral notes.

Liquor: Natural, brilliant green in color with a delicate, smooth, velvety surface. In the cup, it presents a refreshing, aromatic flavor with seductive notes that will delight tea connoisseurs.

Infusion: The stems take on a brilliant green hue with hints of yellow.

PREPARATION

For every 2/3 cup (150 milliliters) of water at 175°F (80°C), use approximately 1/16 oz (2-3 grams) of tea and steep for about 2-3 minutes.

Recommended with: Rice, Vegetables, Cheeses (Asiago, Fontainebleau), Fish cooked with ginger and lemongrass, As an accompaniment to Sunday brunch.

SENCHA KAGOSHIMA

TYPE: GREEN TEA

AREA OF PROVENANCE: JAPAN, KAGOSHIMA, KOYU

Sencha is Japan's most renowned tea, constituting nearly 80% of the country's tea production, featuring various levels of quality. This tea is characterized by its distinctive fresh aroma, achieved through a unique processing method involving a three-fold steam cooking process.

The finest Senchas are rich in amino acids and vitamin C. The first harvest in April, known as Shincha or "new tea," is considered the best.

This exceptional Sencha tea hails from the Kagoshima prefecture, located at the southernmost tip of Japan. It boasts a fresh flavor profile, less astringent than typical Senchas, bearing a striking resemblance to Gyokuro. Its refreshing qualities make it perfect for enjoying in early summer.

TASTING NOTES

Dry: Long, regularly shaped needle-like jade green leaves, emitting a fresh green grass scent with an aquatic top note.

Liquor: Dark green in color, gentle on the palate, slightly astringent with a mild sweet taste and refreshing floral scents. Its flavor reflects the first warm rays of spring sunshine.

Infusion: Very tender leaves, akin to cooked spinach, with grassy and cooked vegetable notes.

PREPARATION

For every 2/3 cup (150 milliliters) of water at 175°F (80°C), use approximately 1/16 oz (2-3 grams) of tea and steep for about 2 1/2 minutes.

Recommended with: Raw and cooked fish, Mollusks and shellfish, Rice, both raw and cooked vegetables, Fresh delicate cheeses, Light pulse soups, Traditional Japanese azuki bean-based desserts.

CHA NO YU:
THE ANCIENT JAPANESE ART OF TEA MAKING

The Japanese tea ritual has deep connections with the spread of Buddhism. In the twelfth century, a monk named Eisai returned from a trip to China, bringing with him the seeds of the tea plant and introducing the Chinese method of preparing tea, which was prevalent during the Song dynasty. In that era, tea leaves were compressed and then stone-milled into a fine powder. As a result, the drink was created by dissolving the powdered tea rather than steeping it, a technique that is still practiced in Japan today.

Tea quickly gained popularity at the imperial court, and its preparation became widespread in monasteries, where monks used it as an energy drink to stay awake during long hours of meditation. Soon, precise rules for tea-making were established, and even competitions emerged. This development greatly appealed to the feudal lords and warriors who dominated medieval society at the time. These early rituals can be considered the precursors of the Cha No Yu, or Japanese tea ceremony.

In Kyoto, Murata Shuko established a tea room made of four and a half tatami mats, where he formulated the initial rules for Cha No Yu. However, it was only with Master Sen no Rikyu (1522-1591) that the art of tea-making evolved into a true ritual with meticulously defined gestures. The Cha No Yu ceremony focused on Matcha, a finely ground green tea still used today.

Cha No Yu, which translates to "hot tea water" in Japanese, is a ceremony characterized by harmony, respect, purity, and tranquility. The ceremony unfolds in a tea room known as the "place of emptiness," accessible by crossing a garden path paved with flat and irregular stones. The host, along with the guests, kneels on tatami mats. The host dries the tea bowl (chawan) with a silk cloth hanging from their kimono belt. Using a bamboo spatula (chashaku), they place a small amount of powdered green Matcha tea into the bowl. With a bamboo ladle (hishaku), they draw hot water from an iron kettle and pour it into the bowl over the tea. To create the desired "jade froth," the tea is vigorously stirred with a special bamboo whisk (chasen).

The Matcha is now ready to be served to the first guest, and the same ceremony is repeated for each guest, with a small traditional dessert accompanying each cup.

It takes years, even decades, of study to master the art of the Japanese tea ceremony. The masters believe that true success in this art requires a deep understanding of the spirit of tea.

GREEN TEA

MATCHA

TYPE: GREEN TEA

AREA OF PROVENANCE: JAPAN, AICHI, NISHIO

Matcha is a traditional Japanese green tea used in the Cha No Yu tea ceremony. Some of the finest green Matcha teas originate from the pristine region of Nishio in the Aichi prefecture, where tea cultivation dates back to the 1200s. These teas are crafted from leaves that are much greener and more nutrient-rich than those found in other parts of the country.

Matcha stands out as the only tea prepared from powdered leaves, which are dissolved in hot water instead of being infused. This tea boasts superior antioxidant and energy-boosting properties compared to other green teas. Lesser-quality Matcha teas find extensive use in gourmet cooking, particularly in baking.

TASTING NOTES

Dry: The powder is exceptionally fine, displaying a glossy emerald green color with the fragrance of an untouched forest.

Liquor: It exudes a vivid green and cloudy appearance, accompanied by the renowned "jade froth" on the surface, providing a unique tactile sensation as you savor it. Its mildly tangy taste hints at the sweetness of blossoms and leaves, leaving a lingering, slightly bitter aftertaste in the mouth, complemented by subtle notes of herbs and freshly cut hay.

PREPARATION

Place approximately 1/16 oz (1 gram) of tea into the dish. This equates to the tip of a teaspoon or the quantity held by a chashaku, a bamboo spatula. Pour hot water at temperatures ranging from 160°-175° F (70°-80° C) into the dish. Stir vigorously with a "chasen," a bamboo whisk, until a dense foam forms.

Recommended with: Matcha pairs beautifully with caviar, oysters, white chocolate, delicate pastries, egg and mascarpone-based creams, and it is ideal for crafting smoothies and soy milk milkshakes. Additionally, you can sprinkle it over soft cheeses to enhance their flavor.

GREEN TEA

YELLOW TEA

Yellow tea is predominantly cultivated in China's Hunan region, with Jun Shan Island being particularly renowned for its production of authentic yellow tea. The tea-making process shares many similarities with green tea production and originated as an accidental variation of green tea.

Yellow tea is predominantly cultivated in China's Hunan region, with Jun Shan Island being particularly renowned for its production of authentic yellow tea. The tea-making process shares many similarities with green tea production and originated as an accidental variation of green tea.

One of the key distinctions between yellow tea and green tea lies in the intentional yellowing of the tea leaves during processing, achieved through light oxidation. The fundamental techniques employed in yellow tea production encompass heating, rolling, covering, and drying.

In the initial phase, the leaves are subjected to high heat in a cauldron to reduce their moisture content. Subsequently, the leaves are rolled to release their essential oils and give them their characteristic shape, mirroring the initial stages of green tea production. The pivotal step that distinguishes yellow tea involves stacking the leaves in sizable piles and covering them, imparting the distinct yellow hue to the leaves. The final drying phase, a common process across tea types, further enhances the yellow coloration.

It is worth noting that many teas in China are marketed as "yellow tea" even if they do not strictly adhere to the characteristics of true yellow tea. This historical practice can be traced back to the association of the color yellow with imperial power, leading to the use of the term "yellow" for the best crops of green or white tea sent as tributes to the imperial court. Consequently, these superior teas were often referred to as yellow teas.

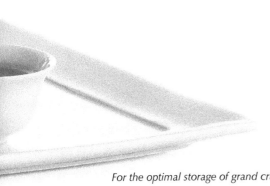

For the optimal storage of grand cru tea leaves, we recommend using airtight containers that protect them from light, moisture and odors.

HOW TO PREPARE
YELLOW TEA

To prepare yellow tea, we recommend using glassware, specifically either a Gaiwan teacup or a tall and narrow glass.

For both methods, it is crucial to ensure that the water temperature falls within the range of 175°-185° F (80°-85° C).

If you opt for a Gaiwan teacup, begin by preheating it. Once heated, fill it approximately one-third full with tea leaves. Depending on your personal preference, you can either steep the tea for a single 3-4 minute infusion or perform multiple, shorter infusions, each lasting around 30-40 seconds.

If you choose to use a tall and narrow glass, start by preheating it as well. Then, add the tea leaves to the glass, filling it around one-third full. Following this, pour in the remaining 70% of hot water. The tea buds will gradually descend to the bottom of the glass, remaining vertical. They will begin to sway gently, creating a captivating visual effect, which this preparation method allows you to fully appreciate.

JUN SHAN YIN ZHEN

TYPE: YELLOW TEA

AREA OF PROVENANCE: CHINA, HUNAN, ISLAND OF JUN SHAN

Jun Shan Yin Zhen yellow tea derives its name from the island of Jun Shan, located in the Hunan region of China, often affectionately called "the island of love" due to its picturesque beauty. This captivating locale is where yellow tea was originally cultivated. Production is exceptionally limited, resulting in high prices. To illustrate the meticulousness of the harvesting process, it takes a minimum of five kilograms of leaves to produce just one kilogram of dry tea.

TASTING NOTES

Dry: The delicate leaves resemble needles and display a uniform appearance, adorned with yellow and silver tips.

Liquor: The infusion has a pale yellow hue with a fresh, enduring aroma reminiscent of flowers and nuts, offering a very soft and velvety texture.

Infusion: The steeped tea, composed of one shoot and one leaf, maintains its brilliant green color and retains its nutty undertones, evoking chestnut and hazelnut flavors.

PREPARATION

Western method: Use approximately 1/16 oz (2-3 grams) of tea for every 2/3 cup (150 milliliters) of water heated to 175-185° F (80-85° C) and steep for 3 minutes.

Eastern method: Employ 1/8 oz (5 grams) of tea for every 2/3 cup (150 milliliters) of water at the same temperature range (175-185° F or 80-85° C) and steep for 3-4 infusions, each lasting 30-40 seconds.

Recommended with: This tea pairs excellently with meals and complements fresh cheeses and white meats.

MENG DING HUANG YA (YELLOW YA)

TYPE: YELLOW TEA

AREA OF PROVENANCE: CHINA, SICHUAN

Meng Ding Huang Ya is an exceptionally rare yellow tea with a rich history dating back over two thousand years. Originating during the Han dynasty, it was later designated as the Imperial tea during the Tang dynasty. This tea is cultivated at the summit of the Meng mountain in Sichuan, an area frequently shrouded in mist, which imparts unique characteristics to the tea leaves. Due to the limited production area, Meng Ding Huang Ya is seldom found outside China, making it a remarkable and exclusive tea for those fortunate enough to encounter it.

Dry: The delicate yellowish leaves have an elegant and uniform appearance.

Liquor: During infusion, the tea shoots remain suspended vertically in the water, creating a graceful dance-like effect. The resulting pale yellow liquor boasts a sweet taste with hints of hazelnuts and herbs.

Infusion: The unfurled leaves reveal the classic composition of high-quality harvests: one shoot and one leaf. Nutty notes of hazelnut and chestnut persistently linger on the palate.

PREPARATION

Western method: Use approximately 1/16 oz (2-3 grams) of tea for every 2/3 cup (150 milliliters) of water heated to 175-185° F (80-85° C) and steep for 3 minutes.

Eastern method: Employ 1/8 oz (5 grams) of tea for every 2/3 cup (150 milliliters) of water at the same temperature range (175-185° F or 80-85° C) and steep for 3-4 infusions, each lasting 30-40 seconds.

Recommended with: This exceptional tea is best savored on its own, allowing its unique flavor to shine. However, it can also be enjoyed alongside light dishes featuring white meats, nuts, and baked pastries.

Ruyao style tea set, appreciated since the times of the Song dynasty
for the characteristic cracks in the surface enamel, considered of great value.

WHITE TEA

In the past, white tea was presented as a tribute to high dignitaries and members of the Chinese court, a testament to its uniqueness and value. The quality of top-rate white tea hinges on several factors, including the botanical specimen used, the processing method employed, and the presence of abundant white down on the tea buds.

Since white tea uses downy shoots and leaves, the resulting pale yellow liquor boasts a velvety smooth mouthfeel and a fresh, full aroma. The preparation of white tea is simple yet special, involving only withering and drying, with no heating or rolling techniques. The most prized variety is composed exclusively of shoots, which are harvested and then placed on shelves in specially ventilated rooms (or exposed to the sun in mild temperatures) until they achieve the desired level of withering. Following this phase, which may take several days, the leaves are dried in large baskets at low temperatures until they are completely dehydrated.

While native to the Fujian region of China, top-quality white tea is also produced in limited quantities outside of China, such as in Ruhuna, in southern Sri Lanka.

HOW TO PREPARE WHITE TEA

For the optimal preparation of white tea, we recommend using a glass or porcelain Gaiwan cup.

It's essential to use water heated to a temperature between 165°F and 175°F (75°C and 80°C). You should also take care to pre-warm the cup, empty it, and then fill it one-third of the way with water heated to the desired temperature for the first infusion. Afterward, add the tea leaves and fill the cup completely with more hot water.

If you prefer a brew with a more distinct and intense taste, opt for a single infusion lasting around 5-10 minutes. Alternatively, you can perform up to 3 brief infusions, each lasting around 30-60 seconds if you prefer a fresher, lighter, and more delicate taste.

White tea requires longer infusion times compared to other types of tea because it is not processed by rolling. During the infusion, the aromas and essential oils within the tea leaves are not immediately released, necessitating longer steeping times.

To fully appreciate all the subtle and delicate nuances of the aromas in this tea category, the Eastern method of infusion with repeated steepings is preferable over the single European infusion.

BAI HAO YIN ZHEN

TYPE: WHITE TEA

AREA OF PROVENANCE: CHINA, FUJIAN, FUDING

Bai Hao Yin Zhen, also known as "silver needle," is a highly regarded white tea produced in the Fujian province of China. Among the most prized white teas, it is made exclusively with unopened tea shoots, representing the pinnacle of white tea craftsmanship.

The best harvests, meticulously performed by hand, come from the mountainous plantations of Tai Lao, in the Fuding region where the original white tea Yin Zhen was first produced. This area enjoys a mild sub-tropical climate characterized by high humidity year-round and abundant rainfall. These ideal climatic conditions promote the growth of this natural wonder, resulting in a crystal-clear, velvety infusion with hints of honey and a subtle floral flavor. Bai Hao Yin Zhen has a long history of being considered a unique and exceptional tea. Traditionally, a portion of the harvest was set aside as a tribute to the Emperor. To this day, it remains one of the most highly prized and expensive teas in existence. The careful selection of unopened tea shoots and the delicacy of its aroma make it a tea for true connoisseurs. Only a refined and experienced palate can fully appreciate the nuanced taste of this tea. It is a tea meant for contemplation, best enjoyed on its own without the distraction of food.

TASTING NOTES

Dry: The tea consists of large, unopened shoots covered with silvery down, as soft to the touch as edelweiss petals.
Liquor: The liquor is pale yellow, offering a soft, velvety texture and a perfect balance of very delicate aromas that harmoniously blend together.
Infusion: The young shoots turn light green during the infusion.

PREPARATION

Western method: Use approximately 1/16 oz (2-3 grams) of tea for every 2/3 cup (150 milliliters) of water heated to 165-175°F (75-80°C). Steep for 5-10 minutes.
Eastern method: Use 1/8 oz (5 grams) of tea for every 150 milliliters of water heated to 165-175°F (75-80°C). Perform up to 3 infusions, each lasting 30-60 seconds.

Recommended with: This tea is best enjoyed on its own, as its delicate flavor is best appreciated without any accompanying food.

WHITE TEA

BAI MU DAN

TYPE: WHITE TEA

AREA OF PROVENANCE: CHINA, FUJIAN, ZHENG HE

Bai Mu Dan, also known as White Peony, is a white tea characterized by its one shoot and two open leaves, offering a more robust and intense flavor compared to other delicate white teas. It originates from the plantations in Zheng He, located in the Fujian province, where Bai Mu Dan was originally cultivated. This tea is notable for its soft, honeyed aroma and the intensity of its velvety, lingering flavor.

TASTING NOTES

Dry: Bai Mu Dan consists of large, unopened shoots covered with dense silvery down, along with open down-covered leaves.

Liquor: The tea produces a pale yellow liquor with delicate, floral, fresh, and velvety notes that hint at honey. In contrast to Bai Hao Yin Zhen, Bai Mu Dan has a stronger, more intense, and lingering taste.

Infusion: The leaves and shoots take on a light green color during infusion.

PREPARATION

Western method: Use approximately 1/16 oz (2-3 grams) of tea for every 2/3 cup (150 milliliters) of water heated to 165-175°F (75-80°C). Steep for 5-10 minutes.

Eastern method: Use 1/8 oz (5 grams) of tea for every 2/3 cup (150 milliliters) of water heated to 165-175°F (75-80°C). Perform up to 3 infusions, each lasting 30-60 seconds.

Recommended with: Bai Mu Dan is ideal for enjoying on its own as a tea for meditation. It also pairs well with light vegetable-based meals, white meats, fish, or fresh and semi-soft cheeses such as Asiago.

RUHUNA SILVER TIPS

TYPE: WHITE TEA

AREA OF PROVENANCE: SRI LANKA, RUHUNA, MATARA DISTRICT

Silver Tips is one of Sri Lanka's finest teas and a source of national pride. Traditionally reserved for kings and tea connoisseurs, this tea is meticulously crafted. It features hand-harvested leaves, with a focus on selecting only unopened shoots. The prime buds are typically harvested from March to May, and the leaves undergo minimal oxidation, primarily through sun drying, without the use of mechanical drying methods. Despite being classified as a white tea, Silver Tips possesses a unique character with delicate balsamic and spicy undertones, reminiscent of classic white teas from Sri Lanka.

TASTING NOTES

Dry: The large shoots are extremely soft, covered in velvety silvery-white down, and emit an intense honey-like fragrance.

Liquor: The liquor is intense yellow with a tendency toward golden brown in prolonged infusions. It is known for its fresh and delicate aroma, distinctive flavor with pronounced honey notes, and a subtle hint of pine. It feels like pure silk on the palate.

Infusion: The large, blemish-free shoots tend to turn white during infusion, releasing honeyed and empyreumatic (aromatic, smoky) notes.

PREPARATION

Western method: Use approximately 1/8 oz (3-5 grams) of tea for every 2/3 cup (150 milliliters) of water heated to 175°F (80°C). Steep for 5-7 minutes.

Recommended with: Silver Tips is best enjoyed on its own to savor its sublime taste. However, it can also be paired with light dishes based on white meats, blue-veined cheeses, or fish.

BLUE-GREEN OR
WULONG TEA - CHINA

Yi Xing terracotta teapot. With use, its porous surface absorbs the aromas of the teas and, in time, enhances the fragrance of quality teas.

This family of teas, better known as Wulong teas (also spelled Oolong, which in Chinese means "black dragon"), comprises a series of teas whose leaves undergo partial oxidation during processing. Different types of products may be obtained, each with unique organoleptic characteristics, depending on the desired intensity.

Low levels of oxidation produce Wulongs similar to green tea, with distinct floral notes.

High levels of oxidation, on the other hand, produce decidedly darker and fruitier Wulongs, very similar to red tea.

These teas originate in the Chinese province of Fujian, where they were first produced around 400 years ago. To this day, the most traditional Wulongs come from this region, as well as Guangdong and Taiwan.

The Wulong of Fujian is produced both in the north and south of the province and is represented by the Wuyi Yan Cha and Anxi Tie Guan Yin varieties. The Fenghuang Dancong botanical specimen is typical of Guangdong, while the Taiwan Wulongs are obtained by processing the Bao Zhong specimen.

The production of Wulong teas is a complex matter: leaves are left to wither in the sun, then air-dried, rotated, heated, rolled, and finally dried once more. The production process is basically a combination of the processes used for the production of green and oxidized teas.

Freshly picked leaves are scattered on canvases and exposed to sunlight to allow part of their moisture to evaporate. This drying process is also called sun withering. Next, air-drying phases – during which the leaves are spread in workshops over bamboo baskets, to release the heat – are alternated with phases of rotation, performed either manually or with the aid of machinery. This process causes friction between the leaves, darkening their edges.

Once the desired level of oxidation has been reached, the leaves are heated to block the enzyme activity responsible for oxidation.

Next, various rolling methods may be applied, depending on the type of Wulong required. Rotary movements release essential oils from the leaves and help to give them their typical rolled or twisted shape. At this point, the leaves are ready for the final drying phase, initially conducted at a high temperature for a short period of time, and then at a low temperature for a decidedly longer time.

There are many legends concerning the origins of Wulong tea and its name, which in Chinese means black dragon. However, they all relate to the accidental discovery of partial oxidation caused by the momentary abandonment, for one reason or another, of the harvested tea leaves.

HOW TO PREPARE WULONG TEA

The best accessories to prepare Wulong tea are a porcelain Gaiwan teacup and a terracotta Yi Xing teapot. One drawback of a porcelain Gaiwan teacup is that it is a good conductor of heat. High-temperature water, around 195-205° F (90-95° C), will quickly overheat the cup's lid, posing a risk of burning your fingers. If you are not familiar with using a Gaiwan teacup, it is better to opt for a terracotta Yi Xing teapot.

The method of preparation practiced in China and Taiwan is the Gong Fu Cha technique. Even today, this ritual is scarcely known in the West, yet it is undoubtedly the best way to appreciate the aromas because it allows the tea leaves to release and express their entire potential for each infusion.

SHORT LESSON IN GONG FU CHA

1. Heat the water to 195-205° F (90-95° C). For Wulong teas that have a low oxidation or for teas whose leaves are not curled, the water must have a slightly lower temperature of around 185-195° F (85-90° C).

2. Place the equipment on the ceremonial table along with the tray to catch liquids. This includes the terracotta teapot, jar, and teacups (the set is composed of a tall cup to experience the scent and a short cup to taste the tea).

3. Pour the water into the teapot to heat it.

4. Pour the water into the jar to heat it.

5. Put the tea leaves into the teapot (around 1/4 or 1/3 the volume of the teapot) using the wooden tea measuring spoon. To more easily add the leaves into the teapot, it might be useful to use the wooden funnel.

6. Pour water into the teapot and briefly rinse the leaves for around 10 seconds. Then empty the teapot and discard the rinse water. This step only serves to wet and soften the leaves to better prepare them for future infusions that you will drink.

7. Once the teapot is filled, close it with the lid. Wait around 30-40 seconds, continuing to pour hot water onto the teapot to prevent it from cooling.

8. Pour the brew from the pot into the jar. During this step, it might be useful to use the strainer to avoid that leaves or parts of leaves are poured into the cups.

9. Pour the brew into the tall aromatizing cups, and then into the short tasting cups. Smell the cup for its aroma, as even if it is empty it will release all of the tea's fragrance. Then taste the tea, drinking the entire contents of the short cup in three small sips.

Wulong teas yield up to 5-7 infusions. Each infusion will be different from the others, creating a more delicate or more intense brew. We recommend that you take the time to experiment, as the goal of the Gong Fu Cha method is to prepare tea in the best way possible.

DA HONG PAO

TYPE: WULONG TEA

AREA OF PROVENANCE: CHINA, FUJIAN, WUYI SHAN

Da Hong Pao is the most renowned among the Wulong teas hailing from the mountainous region of WuYi Shan, situated north of Fujian.

This area, safeguarded by UNESCO, also yields Yan Cha rock teas, with Da Hong Pao reigning as the supreme variety, earning it the title of "the king of WuYi Shan." This iconic tea originates from clones propagated from cuttings of four ancestral parent plants, tracing their lineage back to the Ming dynasty. Every year, only a small quantity of tea leaves is meticulously harvested and processed from these four plants. The scarcity of this tea is reflected in its astronomical price, commanding tens of thousands of dollars per kilogram, making it a true luxury item reserved for a privileged few. This mountain-grown tea boasts a robust body and an enchanting aroma, capable of delivering 8-10 steepings. Undoubtedly, it is a must-try for aficionados of Wulong teas.

TASTING NOTES

Dry: The dark brown, large leaves are lightly rolled lengthwise.
Liquor: Exhibiting a dark orange hue, this tea presents a rounded mouthfeel with a multifaceted bouquet characterized by harmoniously balanced notes of fruit, spices, flowers, leather, sandalwood, and tobacco.
Infusion: The leaves take on very dark shades of brown and black.

PREPARATION

Western method: Use approximately 1/16 oz (2-3 grams) of tea for every 2/3 cup (150 milliliters) of water heated to 195-205°F (90-95°C), steeping for 5 minutes.
Eastern method: Employ 1/8 oz (5 grams) of tea for every 2/3 cup (150 milliliters) of water at a temperature of 195-205°F (90-95°C). Infuse for up to 8-10 brief infusions, each lasting 30-50 seconds. Initiate the process with a swift rinse of the tea leaves.

Recommended with: Da Hong Pao complements red meats, spicy dishes, salty foods (e.g., cold cuts), smoked fish, and pasta featuring meat or vegetable fillings.

FENG HUANG DAN CONG

TYPE: WULONG TEA

AREA OF PROVENANCE: CHINA, GUANGDONG, CHAOZHOU

In contrast to most Wulong teas, Feng Huang Dan Cong does not hail from Fujian but originates from the neighboring region of Guangdong. As is typical in China, the origins of the most prized and expensive teas are veiled in mystery. Translated from Chinese, the tea's name means "tree of the Feng Huang mountains." This tea is meticulously harvested from colossal ancient tea plants that flourish in a forest housing a minimum of 3,000 plants, all aged over a century. The most elderly plants, with just one or two branches that still produce leaves, are a testament to the scarcity of this low-oxidation Wulong tea. Each harvest yields only limited quantities of tea, with each possessing unique characteristics. It wasn't until the early 1960s that a novel cultivation method emerged, offering characteristics strikingly similar to those of centuries-old plants while significantly enhancing productivity.

TASTING NOTES
Dry: The light green-beige leaves are gently rolled lengthwise.
Liquor: Radiating a golden yellow hue, this tea boasts a dense, velvety, and nearly oily flavor profile. It unfolds with intense floral notes and hints of exotic fruit, alongside the essence of ripe, spiced peaches.
Infusion: The sizable leaves take on a matte green appearance with touches of red along the edges.

PREPARATION
Western method: Utilize approximately 1/16 oz (2-3 grams) of tea for every 2/3 cup (150 milliliters) of water heated to 185-195°F (85-90°C), steeping for 5 minutes.
Eastern method: Employ 1/8 oz (5 grams) of tea for every 2/3 cup (150 milliliters) of water at a temperature of 185-195°F (85-90°C). Infuse for up to 5-6 brief infusions, each lasting 30-40 seconds. Commence the process with a quick rinse of the tea leaves.

Recommended with: Feng Huang Dan Cong pairs well with lightly salted dishes, spicy cuisine, shellfish, tempura-fried fish or vegetables, pork, fresh cheeses, fruit, apple pie, and milk or white chocolate.

HUANG JIN GUI

TYPE: WULONG TEA

AREA OF PROVENANCE: CHINA, FUJIAN, ANXI

Huang Jin Gui Wulong tea hails from Anxi, Fujian, and is often considered the lesser-known "cousin" of the globally recognized Tie Guan Yin tea. Crafted from the Huang Dan tea plant variety, it undergoes mild oxidation using processes akin to Tie Guan Yin, resulting in its distinctive floral notes. With origins tracing back to the Qing dynasty, this tea holds a significant place in Chinese tea history. Although overshadowed by the success of Tie Guan Yin in recent decades, it has experienced a resurgence of attention and appreciation in recent years.

Huang Jin Gui is an excellent choice for afternoon tea or to complement meals.

TASTING NOTES
Dry: The light green leaves are tightly rolled into small pearl shapes.
Liquor: Exhibiting a pale golden yellow hue, it bursts with floral notes (osmanthus), butter, and vanilla, providing a velvety texture to the palate.
Infusion: The brilliantly green, rolled leaves are large and consistently shaped.

PREPARATION
Western method: Use approximately 1/16 oz (2-3 grams) of tea for every 2/3 cup (150 milliliters) of water heated to 185-195°F (85-90°C), steeping for 5 minutes.
Eastern method: Employ 1/8 oz (5 grams) of tea for every 2/3 cup (150 milliliters) of water at 185-195°F (85-90°C). Infuse for up to 5-6 brief infusions lasting 20-40 seconds each, starting with a quick rinse of the leaves.

Recommended with: Huang Jin Gui pairs beautifully with lightly salted foods, shellfish, and cheeses such as brie and camembert. It also complements fruit, particularly strawberries.

SHUI XIAN - WATER SPRITE

TYPE: WULONG TEA

AREA OF PROVENANCE: CHINA, FUJIAN, WUYI SHAN

Shui Xian and Tie Guan Yin are highly popular Wulong tea varieties in China and are favored choices for the Gong Fu Cha tea ceremony. Shui Xian tea, often indicated by the "Shui Hsien" character, originates from the high mountains of WuYi Shan, synonymous with high-quality Wulong tea.

Wulong teas from the WuYi mountains are also known as "Yan Cha" or "Tea rock," owing to the rocky terrain in and around the tea gardens. Rich in mineral salts, Shui Xian offers a robust Wulong with a full-bodied flavor, culminating in a fresh, fruity, and floral aftertaste. When the quality is less exceptional, toasted and woody notes tend to dominate. Shui Xian tea leaves are notably larger than those of other Wulong teas.

TASTING NOTES

Dry: The tea boasts long leaves traditionally rolled and, due to a high degree of oxidation, appear dark anthracite in color.

Liquor: Displaying a bronze hue, high-quality Shui Xian teas strike a harmonious balance between smoked, woody, fruity, and orchid notes, leaving a delightful and enduring impression on the palate.

Infusion: The leaves are exceptionally large and leathery.

PREPARATION

Western method: Utilize approximately 1/16 oz (2-3 grams) of tea for every 2/3 cup (150 milliliters) of water heated to 190-205°F (90-95°C), steeping for 5 minutes.

Eastern method: Employ 1/8 oz (5 grams) of tea for every 2/3 cup (150 milliliters) of water at 190-205°F (90-95°C). Infuse for up to 5-6 rounds, each lasting 30-60 seconds, and initiate the process with a brief rinse of the leaves.

Recommended with: Shui Xian tea complements red meats, soft pressed cheeses such as Gruyere or Emmental, as well as pasta dishes with meat or vegetarian fillings.

TIE GUAN YIN

TYPE: WULONG TEA

AREA OF PROVENANCE: CHINA, FUJIAN, ANXI

Tie Guan Yin is a prominent star in the Gong Fu Cha tea ceremony and stands as the most renowned Chinese Wulong tea. It originates from Anxi in the Fujian region, where its cultivation has been rooted for millennia. This tea is distinguished by its mere 10-15% oxidation, imparting vibrant, floral notes. It boasts a lack of astringency, exceptional thirst-quenching attributes, and a low tannin content, making it an excellent choice for any time of day. Its intense aroma and absence of a lingering aftertaste refresh the palate and elevate the flavors of food, making Tie Guan Yin the perfect interlude between courses. Over the past few decades, the soaring popularity of this tea has led to widespread production, albeit often far from its original terroir.

TASTING NOTES

Dry: The tea features brilliant green leaves tightly rolled into pearls.

Liquor: It presents a golden, oily appearance and an incredibly soft, velvety texture. The tea is characterized by a rich, persistent, and intoxicating floral bouquet, including hints of jasmine, magnolia, orchid, lily of the valley, wisteria, and wildflowers.

Infusion: The leaves are notably large and exhibit a dark green hue.

PREPARATION

Western method: Use approximately 1/16 oz (2-3 grams) of tea for every 2/3 cup (150 milliliters) of water heated to 185-195°F (85-90°C), steeping for 4 minutes.

Eastern method: Employ approximately 1/8 oz (5-6 grams) of tea for every 2/3 cup (150 milliliters) of water at 185-195°F (85-90°C). Infuse for up to 5-7 rounds, each lasting 30-40 seconds, with a quick rinse of the leaves before beginning.

Recommended with: Tie Guan Yin pairs wonderfully with spicy foods, lightly salted vegetable-based dishes, rice, or white meats. It also shines when enjoyed with a snack of oven-baked delicacies.

The glass jug and small tasting cup are essential accessories when preparing
Wulong tea following the Gong Fu Cha method

BLUE-GREEN OR WULONG TEA - TAIWAN

Taiwan has gained recognition for producing some of the finest Wulong teas globally. The first tea plants, originally hailing from the Chinese province of Fujian, were introduced to northern Taiwan towards the end of the 1700s. This region enjoys a mild and humid climate, with summer temperatures below 82°F (28°C) and winter temperatures above 55°F (13°C), along with substantial rainfall – ideal conditions for cultivating high-quality Wulong tea.

Historically, tea cultivation in this area primarily targeted exports, especially to the United States and Japan. In fact, during the early 1980s, around 80% of Taiwan's tea production was exported. However, in recent years, producers have shifted their focus towards the local market, recognizing the potential for high-quality tea. Significant efforts have been made to produce exceptional teas, including Grand Cru and organic varieties.

Taiwan's semi-oxidized Wulong teas can be categorized into three main groups: low-oxidation teas (e.g., Bao Zhong), pearl-shaped rolled teas (e.g., Ding Dong, Jin Xuan, and scented Osmanthus and Bergamot teas), and high-oxidation teas (e.g., Bai Hao Wulong). The primary production areas include Nantou and Taipei counties, along with the villages of Beipu and Emei in the north-west of the island, as well as the Ali Shan mountains.

BAO ZHONG

TYPE: WULONG TEA

AREA OF PROVENANCE: TAIWAN, NANTOU, AOWANDA

This blue-green tea hails from the county of Nantou and thrives in mountain gardens at an altitude of approximately 4,595 feet (1,400 meters). Bao Zhong is a specialty of the north and central regions of the island. Thanks to its delightful taste, it has gained popularity not only in Taiwan but also in China and Europe. Currently, production of this tea is on the rise.

The dark green leaves undergo 20% oxidation, resulting in a light and fresh liquor reminiscent of green tea. The aroma is unmistakable yet subtle, followed by a sweet aftertaste. Its low tannin content makes it a versatile tea suitable for any time of day.

TASTING NOTES

Dry: Very large, dark green open leaves, lightly rolled along their length.

Liquor: Pale golden yellow; in the mouth, the tea is very sweet, fresh, and exhibits floral notes like jasmine and rose.

Infusion: The leaves are dark green, tending to brown at the edges.

PREPARATION

Western method: Use approximately 1/16 oz (2-3 grams) for every 2/3 cup (150 milliliters) of water at 185-195°F (85-90°C) for a 5-minute infusion.

Eastern method: Use 1/8 oz (5 grams) for every 2/3 cup (150 milliliters) of water at 185-195°F (85-90°C) for up to 4-5 infusions of 20-30 seconds each, preceded by a quick rinse of the leaves.

Recommended with: Bao Zhong pairs well with lightly salted foods, spicy dishes, fish, poultry, eggs, pork, vegetables, sweets with honey, sweet and savory crêpes, fruit salad (also excellent when served cold with fruit).

DONG DING

TYPE: WULONG TEA

AREA OF PROVENANCE: TAIWAN, NANTOU, AOWANDA

This classic Wulong tea, one of Taiwan's finest, is named after the Dong Ding mountain in the Nantou region. The tea gardens are situated at an altitude of 1400 meters in an incredibly beautiful natural setting known for its maple forests, which burst into vibrant colors every autumn. In Chinese, "Dong Ding" translates to "icy peak," a reference to the mountain where tea cultivation has been practiced since the late 19th century, with tea plants originating from the WuYi Shan mountain range in Fujian, China.

Dong Ding Wulong undergoes 30% oxidation, resulting in a sweet, fresh, and highly aromatic tea. Its low tannin content makes it an ideal choice for afternoon or evening consumption.

TASTING NOTES

Dry: Tightly rolled leaves with an intense dark green color.
Liquor: The cup reveals a dark yellow liquor with a distinctive aroma featuring top notes of leather and tobacco that gradually transition into intense floral-vanilla notes.
Infusion: The open leaves are notably large.

PREPARATION

Western method: Use approximately 1/16 oz (2-3 grams) for every 2/3 cup (150 milliliters) of water at 195-205°F (90-95°C) for a 5-minute infusion.
Eastern method: Use 1/8 oz (5 grams) for every 2/3 cup (150 milliliters) of water at 195-205°F (90-95°C) for up to 5-7 infusions of 30-40 seconds each, preceded by a quick rinse of the leaves.

Recommended with: Dong Ding tea is highly versatile. Its sweet vanilla notes complement lemon biscuits, crème caramel, and chocolate. Its mildness pairs well with spicy foods, blue-veined cheeses, salmon, carpaccio, and lamb.

HIGH MOUNTAIN JIN XUAN (MILKY WULONG)

TYPE: WULONG TEA

AREA OF PROVENANCE: TAIWAN, NANTOU, AOWANDA

The garden where this tea is cultivated is nestled in the Nantou region, perched at an elevation of 4,595 feet (1,400 meters). This tea undergoes a 20% oxidation process and is derived from a new plant variety developed for Dong Ding cultivation. However, what sets apart this equally renowned Oolong tea, the High Mountain Jin Xuan, is its distinct buttery and milky notes, earning it the moniker Milky Oolong.

TASTING NOTES

Dry: Yellow-green leaves, tightly rolled into pearls.

Liquor: Crystal clear, golden-yellow; soft and velvety, devoid of astringency with pronounced confectionery notes (caramel, butter, condensed milk); delicate and enduring flavor.

Infusion: Large, light green leaves; characterized by floral notes.

PREPARATION

Western method: Use approximately 1/16 oz (2-3 grams) of tea for every 2/3 cup (150 milliliters) of water at 195°F (90°C) for a 5-minute infusion.

Eastern method: Use approximately 1/8 oz (5-6 grams) of tea for every 2/3 cup (150 milliliters) of water at 195°F (90°C) for up to 5-7 infusions, each lasting 20-40 seconds. Begin with a quick rinse of the leaves.

Recommended with: Enjoy with apple pie, pastries, or crème brûlée.

ORIENTAL BEAUTY

TYPE: WULONG TEA

AREA OF PROVENANCE: TAIWAN, NANTOU, AOWANDA

This summer tea, oxidized to 60%, thrives in gardens situated at an altitude of approximately 4,595 feet (1,400 meters) in the Nantou region. Oriental Beauty, a variety of Bai Hao, which translates to "white tip," stands as Taiwan's most renowned Wulong tea.

What lends this tea its unique character is a specific occurrence: the leaves are exclusively harvested during the summer after tiny insects known as jassids have graced the gardens, nibbling on the leaves. These insects are perceived as nature's helpers, for their gentle nibbling breaks the leaf edges and initiates oxidation in the living leaves still attached to the branches. After processing, the leaves acquire a reddish-brown hue with distinctive white tips. The insects' labor also imparts a characteristic delicate aroma of honey and peaches. This tea was previously known as Formosa Wulong until Queen Elizabeth II, charmed right from her first sip of this extraordinary tea, renamed it Oriental Beauty.

TASTING NOTES

Dry: Full-bodied, dark brown leaves with silvery shoots and fruity, spicy undertones.
Liquor: A brilliant amber hue; it offers fruity notes (fig, plum, and cherry), with peach taking the lead, accompanied by hints of honey, vanilla, spices (cinnamon and licorice), and wild orchid, leaving a lingering aftertaste.
Infusion: The leaves bear evident signs of insect bites; the fruity, spicy notes persist, with a touch of woodiness.

PREPARATION

Western method: Utilize approximately 1/16 oz (2-3 grams) of tea for every 2/3 cup (150 milliliters) of water at 195-205°F (90-95°C) for a 5-minute infusion.
Eastern method: Opt for around 1/8 oz (5-6 grams) of tea for every 2/3 cup (150 milliliters) of water at 195-205°F (90-95°C) for up to 6-7 infusions, each lasting 30-40 seconds. Commence with a quick rinse of the leaves.

Recommended with: Oriental Beauty complements pulse soups, seasoned cheeses, spicy foods, pork, smoked fish, and cold cuts.

BERGAMOT WULONG

TYPE: SCENTED WULONG TEA

AREA OF PROVENANCE: TAIWAN, NANTOU, AOWANDA

Produced in the finest gardens of Nantou, Bergamot Wulong achieves a harmonious balance between the floral and fruity notes characteristic of high mountain Wulongs and the subtle citrus hints from fresh bergamot flowers. The delicate natural fragrance arises from the fusion of freshly processed tea leaves with these fragrant flowers. The result is bound to captivate you and leave you questioning the hype surrounding Earl Grey. This tea undergoes 15% oxidation.

TASTING NOTES

Dry: Dark green leaves with yellow tips, tightly rolled, accompanied by stalks and a sprinkling of bergamot zest.
Liquor: A clear, golden yellow infusion with a slight astringency. Citrus and floral notes take center stage, followed by a delicate honeydew aftertaste.
Infusion: Large dark green leaves intermingled with fine fragments of bergamot peel.

PREPARATION

Western method: Employ approximately 1/16 oz (2-3 grams) of tea for every 2/3 cup (150 milliliters) of water at 185-195°F (85-90°C) for a 5-minute infusion.
Eastern method: Opt for around 1/8 oz (5-6 grams) of tea for every 2/3 cup (150 milliliters) of water at 185-195°F (85-90°C) for up to 5-7 infusions, each lasting 20-40 seconds. Begin with a quick rinse of the leaves.

Recommended with: Bergamot Wulong pairs wonderfully with shellfish, both dark and white chocolate, lightly salted foods, carbohydrates, and fruit.

OSMANTHUS WULONG

TYPE: SCENTED WULONG TEA

AREA OF PROVENANCE: TAIWAN, NANTOU, AOWANDA

This exquisite "nectar" hails from the Nantou region, renowned for producing some of Taiwan's most highly regarded teas. The tea undergoes a minimal oxidation process of 12-15% after being harvested from plantations nestled 1,400 meters above sea level. The delicate osmanthus flower aroma, highly treasured in the East, is employed to infuse Wulong, green, and red teas. This evergreen plant, belonging to the Oleaceae family, boasts white-yellow blossoms with a robust fragrance reminiscent of magnolia, gardenia, and freesia. The scent is transferred naturally by contact, following a similar method to that of jasmine teas. Repeated contact between tea leaves and fresh osmanthus flowers continues until the perfect balance between the fruity essence of Wulong and the floral aroma of osmanthus is achieved. Ideal for those who relish fresh Wulong and lightly oxidized teas.

TASTING NOTES

Dry: Yellow-green leaves, tightly rolled.

Liquor: A crystal-clear, golden yellow infusion that is soft, velvety, and devoid of astringency. Dominated by top floral notes complemented by delicate yet enduring fruity undertones.

Infusion: Large, light green leaves tinged with dark red edges.

PREPARATION

Western method: Employ approximately 1/16 oz (2-3 grams) of tea for every 2/3 cup (150 milliliters) of water at 185-195°F (85-90°C) for a 5-minute infusion.

Eastern method: Opt for around 1/8 oz (5-6 grams) of tea for every 2/3 cup (150 milliliters) of water at 185-195°F (85-90°C) for up to 5-7 infusions, each lasting 20-40 seconds. Commence with a quick rinse of the leaves.

Recommended with: Osmanthus Wulong pairs beautifully with fish and vegetable tempura, sweet and savory crêpes, fruit, and white chocolate.

*The dual-chamber glass cups isolate heat,
making it easier to enjoy teas requiring
high infusion temperatures, like red teas.*

RED TEA

According to the Chinese color classification, red teas are what are commonly known as black teas in the West. The dark color of these teas, which led to their being called black by the British, is due to the high level of oxidation (not fermentation, as is often erroneously stated) to which the leaves are subjected during processing.

The basic stages of production include withering, rolling, oxidation, and drying. During the first phase, the fresh leaves are spread out on racks and left to wither. This reduces their moisture by up to 60% and makes them softer and easier to process, preventing breakage during subsequent manipulations. Rolling serves to release the leaves' essential oils and give them the desired shape.

At this point, a process of oxidation, performed through enzyme activity, causes the tea leaves to turn "red." This is the most crucial step in the processing of red tea. The leaves are spread out on racks to air dry, obtaining their distinctive aroma and the typical color of oxidized tea. This red hue darkens further during the final drying phase, prior to storage, as the degree of hydration of the leaves reduces further.

Various classifications are used to indicate these completely oxidized teas. In this book, we will use the following criteria:

1. The term "red tea" will be used to refer to tea from China and Taiwan.
2. In line with the most widespread terminology, the term "black tea" will be used to refer to all teas from other Asian countries, such as black Indian tea, black Sri Lankan tea, etc.

The dark red color typical of the liquor of oxidised teas is due to their particular production process.

CHINESE RED TEA

Chinese red tea is traditionally grown in the regions of Anhui, Yunnan, and Fujian. The world-renowned Qimen tea – a favorite with the British monarchy – comes from the city of Qimen, in the Anhui province. The well-informed report that this is the tea the Queen loves best and is prepared for her birthday celebrations.

Qimen and Dian Hong, from the mountains of southwestern Yunnan, undoubtedly share the title of the best Chinese red teas. This region offers the ideal climatic and geological conditions for the cultivation of high-quality teas. These red teas have complex bouquets, with perfectly balanced notes of flowers, cocoa, leather, and cooked fruit.

Another famous tea, produced mainly for Western markets, is Zheng Shan Xiao Zhong, a smoked tea better known by the name of Lapsang Souchong. This tea, referred to by the Chinese as the "tea for Westerners," comes from the mountainous areas of WuYi Shan, in Fujian.

HOW TO PREPARE RED TEA

To prepare red teas, we recommend using porcelain, glass, or terracotta teapots. If you are a great admirer of red Yunnan or smoked teas, you should designate one terracotta teapot specifically to prepare teas in this family. The porousness of the terracotta, over time, will continue to improve your tea set.

Use water that is between 195-205°F (90-95°C). According to your personal taste, you can do one 3-4 minute infusion or 4-5 brief infusions that are around 40 seconds each.

For either case, heat the teapot by filling it with boiling water. This water will be discarded before adding the tea leaves and proceeding with the infusion.

The ideal quantity is around 1/8 oz (6 grams, around one heaping tablespoon of tea leaves) for every 1 1/4 cups or 300 ml.

You do not have to briefly rinse the leaves before proceeding with the first infusion.

LAPSANG SOUCHONG - ZHENG SHAN XIAO ZHONG

TYPE: SCENTED RED TEA

AREA OF PROVENANCE: CHINA, FUJIAN, TONG MU

Zheng Shan Xiao Zhong (small leaf variety) is the real name of this very special red tea that is smoked with pine wood. More famous in the West than in its motherland, the original Lapsang Souchong comes from Tong Mu, a small village that sits amidst the WuYi Shan mountains in Fujian. Here, the Jiang family boasts of having created this special tea in the times of the Ming dynasty and of having produced it for more than 24 generations.

With its smoky taste, there is no in-between: it is either loved by aficionados or hated for its very particular bitter taste. The smoky notes completely smother the aromas in the leaves. For this reason, it is produced using the Souchong, a very large leaf which has little aromatic content and a low level of tannin.

TASTING NOTES
Dry: The dark anthracite grey leaves have very intense empyreumatic notes resembling bacon.
Liquor: The liquor is amber in color, and it is a strong tea with very noticeable smoky notes that linger on the palate.
Infusion: The leaves turn brown, tending towards beige, during the infusion.

PREPARATION
Approx. 1/16 oz (2-3 grams) for every 2/3 cup (150 milliliters) of water at 205°F (95°C) for a 3-minute infusion.

Recommended with: perfect with brunch, large fish (tuna, cod), game, flavored cheeses, eggs, or used as a "spice" instead of pancetta in vegetarian recipes.

QIMEN

TYPE: RED TEA

AREA OF PROVENANCE: CHINA, ANHUI, QIMEN

Produced in Qimen in the Anhui region, for many years this was considered the best Chinese red tea. Qimen (English transliteration of Keemun) is a strong tea with a rich aromatic liquor and a delicate scent of orchids. Production only began fairly recently.

In 1876, a retired high functionary from this area, known for the excellence of its tea, introduced the red tea processing technique he had learned while working in Fujian. The result was a great success: this really is the Queen of all teas. While on the subject, well-informed sources say that this tea is a favorite at Buckingham Palace.

TASTING NOTES

Dry: Thin, dark, stubby leaves with a few golden shoots.
Liquor: Brilliant red with aromatic fruity notes and a lingering flavor of orchids. It is soft and velvety, with no astringent characteristics.
Infusion: The dark red leaves emit a scent of cooked fruit, leather, and cocoa.

PREPARATION

Approx. 1/16 oz (2-3 grams) for every 2/3 cup (150 milliliters) of water at 195-205°F (90-95°C) for a 3-minute infusion.

Recommended with: Red meat, soft cheeses like Reblochon, Camembert, Gorgonzola, eggs, and pizza.

GOLDEN YUNNAN

TYPE: RED TEA

AREA OF PROVENANCE: CHINA, YUNNAN, LING YUN

This red tea is made exclusively from golden shoots (from whence it takes its name) from the mountain plantations in the Ling Yun reserve, in the region of Yunnan. This is considered the best Dian Hong from the area. The word Dian is an abbreviation of the name Yunnan while Hong is the Chinese word for red, the color of oxidized teas. The plant variety and a special oxidization process turn the leaves a unique red color which, in the cup, transforms into a delicate fruity, flowery aroma that is typical of the most prized red teas of Yunnan.

A sophisticated tea for breakfast or any other time of day.

TASTING NOTES

Dry: the harvest consists of gathering long golden-tipped shoots covered with a light coat of feathery down.

Liquor: amber-red with a complex yet unique bouquet of harmoniously balanced fruity, flowery, and honeyed notes, with a hint of woodiness.

Infusion: the leaves are a brilliant red-brown in color and well-proportioned.

PREPARATION

Western method: approx. 1/16 oz (2-3 grams) for every 2/3 cup (150 milliliters) of water at 195°F (90°C) for a 2-3-minute infusion.

Eastern method: 1/8 oz (5 grams) for every 2/3 cup (150 milliliters) of water at 195°F (90°C) for up to 4 infusions of 20-40 seconds each.

Recommended with: perfect with a continental breakfast, lightly salted foods, grilled meats, lamb, almond desserts, milk or white chocolate, fruit compotes, and pizza.

RED MAO FENG

TYPE: RED TEA

AREA OF PROVENANCE: CHINA, YUNNAN, LINCANG

Red Mao Feng is one of the most highly prized teas belonging to the Dian Hong category, and is the archetypal Yunnan red tea. This variety consists exclusively of golden shoots with a light down covering, and comes from the mountain plantations in the region of Lincang at 3,280 feet (1,000 meters) above sea level.

After preparation, the liquor is bright red with a sweet taste and a delicate aroma.

A fantastic tea for any time of day.

TASTING NOTES

Dry: The tea has curly golden leaves.

Liquor: In the cup, it presents a lively and brilliant dark red color. The tea releases a delicate flowery and fruity scent with a lingering flavor. Alongside the mature fruit notes, there are hints of malt and cocoa, creating a delicate yet characterful taste.

Infusion: The steeped leaves take on a brilliant red-brown hue during infusion.

PREPARATION

Western method: Use approximately 1/16 oz (2-3 grams) of tea for every 2/3 cup (150 milliliters) of water at 205° F (90° C). Steep for 2-3 minutes.

Eastern method: Use 1/8 oz (5 grams) of tea for every 2/3 cup (150 milliliters) of water at 205° F (90° C). You can steep the tea for up to 4 infusions, with each infusion lasting 20-40 seconds.

Recommended with: This tea pairs well with a continental breakfast, grilled meats, game, smoked fish, almond desserts, milk or white chocolate, fruit compotes, and apple pie.

RED TEA

INDIAN AND SRI LANKAN BLACK TEA

Tea was first produced in India in the nineteenth century. The British had explored the possibility of cultivating tea in their colony using seeds from China. However, their lack of expertise in the matter and the
absence of established know-how led to the project's failure. Robert Bruce also made unsuccessful attempts in
Assam to cultivate a local plant similar to the tea observed in China. The initial crop, sold in Calcutta in 1836,
was of very poor quality. At this juncture, there was only one viable solution: the British Crown dispatched a
botanist named Robert Fortune to China on a covert mission with the objective of acquiring plants, seeds, and,
most importantly, the secrets of large-scale tea cultivation.

In the latter half of the 1800s, production expanded from Assam to Nilgiri and Darjeeling, located near the
Himalayas. Within a few decades, the quantity of Indian tea imported into England exceeded that from China.
The black teas produced in India are not exclusively intended for export but also for local consumption, where
the traditional "chai" is consumed daily. This is a fragrant blend of black teas, spices, sugar, and milk.
The four annual harvests - in spring (March and April), summer (May and June), monsoon time (July-August),
and autumn (October and November) - each offer distinct aromatic notes. The most highly regarded harvests
among connoisseurs are those of spring (first flush) and summer (second flush). First flush harvests yield light,
slightly astringent teas with a floral aroma and hints of nutmeg and green almonds. Second flush harvests feature a fruity nutmeg flavor. They are smoother, more rounded, and full-bodied compared to spring teas.

In the nineteenth century, coffee was extensively cultivated in Sri Lanka. Following a calamity caused by a
parasite, tea cultivation gradually supplanted coffee, making Ceylon the world's second-largest tea producer.
The primary production regions include Galle, Kandy, Nuwara Eliya, Ratnapura, Dimbula, and Uva. Teas are
categorized not only by their area of origin but also by plantation altitude. Consequently, we have high-grown
teas (above 3,937 feet or 1,200 meters), mid-grown teas (between 1,970 and 3,937 feet or 600 and 1,200
meters), and low-grown teas (below 1,970 feet or 600 meters).

HOW TO PREPARE BLACK TEA:
ENGLISH TEA

The guidelines for the art of preparing English tea are as follows:

1. Select mild water, either spring water or water with a low mineral residue, and heat it to a temperature between 195-205°F (90-95°C).

2. Warm the teapot by pouring hot water into it. Allow it to sit for a few moments, then discard the water.

3. Add one teaspoon of tea leaves for each cup, plus an additional one for the teapot.

4. Pour in the heated water and wait approximately 2-3 minutes for first flush Darjeeling, and 3 minutes for other Indian or Sri Lankan teas.

and 3 minutes for other Indian or Singhalese teas;

5. Filter the tea and serve it in white porcelain cups.

The perfect tea time should be accompanied by scones, clotted cream, strawberry jam, tea sandwiches, cakes, and pastries.

The English enjoy their tea with milk and one or two sugar cubes.

DARJEELING CASTLETON FTGFOP1 - SF

TYPE: BLACK TEA

AREA OF PROVENANCE: INDIA, DARJEELING, CASTLETON

This tea is a classic choice for breakfast and proudly bears the title of "Wonder Muscatel," a distinction that highlights the exceptional quality of Darjeeling summer teas known for their rare fruity aroma. The unique fruity notes of this summer tea are initiated by the bite of an insect called jassid, which triggers the oxidation process in the leaves even before they are harvested. Darjeeling Muscatel teas are cherished for their elegant aroma and well-rounded, harmonious flavor.

Situated in the northern Kurseong region, this garden thrives at an altitude ranging from 3,281 to 6,562 feet (1,000 to 2,000 meters). It is one of the most renowned and esteemed tea plantations in the Darjeeling region. Muscatel is an "historic" Indian tea with a production history dating back to the late 19th century.

TASTING NOTES

Dry: The leaves exhibit a dark hazelnut hue with golden tips created by the presence of shoots.

Liquor: The liquor is a rich dark orange with hints of gold. It offers a soft, enveloping character with fruity notes reminiscent of grapes, plums, and citrus fruits, along with floral and woody undertones.

Infusion: The infusion is even and displays a brilliant dark leather color. The fruity, floral, and woody notes tend to linger on the palate.

PREPARATION

For every 2/3 cup (150 milliliters) of water, use approximately 1/16 oz (2-3 grams) of tea leaves. Brew the tea at 195°F (90°C) for approximately 3 minutes.

Recommended with: This tea pairs wonderfully with a continental breakfast, dishes like gnocchi or stuffed pasta, lemon chicken, mushroom quiche, sweet and savory crêpes, orange curd pastries, apple pie, and honey sweets.

BLACK TEA

DARJEELING GOPALDHARA FTGFOP1 - FF

TYPE: BLACK TEA

AREA OF PROVENANCE: INDIA, DARJEELING, GOPALDHARA

The Gopaldhara tea gardens thrive in the picturesque Mirik valley, nestled at an impressive altitude ranging from 5,577 to 7,218 feet (1,700 to 2,200 meters). Gopaldhara claims the distinction of being the highest tea plantation in Darjeeling and the second highest globally. The extreme climate conditions at this lofty altitude lead to a harvest that takes place 4-5 weeks later than usual. The cold environment also imparts a more delicate flavor to the tea compared to those harvested at lower altitudes.

TASTING NOTES

Dry: The tea leaves are notably large, dark green, and tightly rolled, featuring silvery buds. They exude fruity and floral notes complemented by a subtly toasted underlying aroma.

Liquor: The liquor exhibits a slight astringency and boasts a brilliant copper color. It delivers a floral bouquet followed by delightful hints of citrus fruits, almonds, and vanilla, resulting in a unique infusion that captivates all who savor it.

Infusion: The infused leaves primarily display shades of green with a few brown tones.

PREPARATION

For every 2/3 cup (150 milliliters) of water, use approximately 1/16 oz (2-3 grams) of tea leaves. Brew the tea at 185-195°F (85-90°C) for around 3 minutes.

Recommended with: Darjeeling teas, with their tannin notes, make an ideal companion for a continental breakfast and carbohydrate-rich dishes. They also pair perfectly with grilled fish, salmon, cheeses like brie, mozzarella, and camembert, lamb, eggs, and fresh fruit.

DARJEELING JUNGPANA FTGFOP1 - SF WONDER MUSCATEL

TYPE: BLACK TEA
AREA OF PROVENANCE: INDIA, DARJEELING, JUNGPANA

Hidden amidst the Himalayas, the Jungpana tea garden has garnered international acclaim for its tea, renowned for its distinct nutmeg aroma. For over a century, this estate has been producing high-quality tea. The moniker "Wonder Muscatel" signifies the characteristic fruity bouquet reminiscent of nutmeg, which is a hallmark of several Darjeeling summer teas. During the summer, a curious natural phenomenon occurs: insects known as jassids nibble on the tender tea leaves, altering their chemical composition. These nibbles, during the oxidation process, impart particularly fruity and woody notes to the tea. Situated near Darjeeling at an elevation ranging from 3,281 to 4,593 feet (1,000 to 1,400 meters), this plantation enjoys a privileged south-facing position. However, reaching the gardens is challenging, and to this day, local villagers transport the tea downhill in wooden crates.

Tea from the second Jungpana harvest is a delightful morning indulgence, whether enjoyed with or without milk. Its palate-pleasing gentleness is reminiscent of the finest Wulong teas.

🍃 TASTING NOTES
Dry: The tea leaves exhibit a dark hazelnut hue.
Liquor: The liquor possesses an orange hue with hints of gold. It is soft and enveloping, featuring fruity notes reminiscent of grapes and plums, intertwined with floral and woody undertones.
Infusion: The infusion yields a color akin to dark leather, accompanied by enduring floral, fruity, and subtly spicy notes.

🍃 PREPARATION
For every 2/3 cup (150 milliliters) of water, use approximately 1/16 oz (2-3 grams) of tea leaves. Brew the tea at 195°F (90°C) for approximately 3 minutes.

Recommended with: Ideal when paired with a continental breakfast, honey sweets, sweet and savory crêpes, and orange curd pastries.

BLACK TEA

DARJEELING MARGARET'S HOPE FTGFOP1 - FF

TYPE: BLACK TEA

AREA OF PROVENANCE: INDIA, DARJEELING, MARGARET'S HOPE

Nestled amidst the stunning backdrop of the Himalayan peaks lies the Margaret's Hope plantation, one of the most picturesque tea-producing regions in Darjeeling. This area is renowned not only for its natural beauty but also for producing black tea of "champagne" quality, a tradition dating back to 1860. Abundant rainforests, wild orchids, and velvety moss create an ideal environment for cultivating tea in perfect harmony with the ecosystem.

Margaret's Hope offers a first flush variety with soft, beautifully variegated leaves, exemplifying the sophisticated style of this garden. The tea is characterized by a rare flowery taste with delightful almond undertones.

TASTING NOTES

Dry: The tea features brilliant, slightly rounded green leaves adorned with silver tips from small shoots. It exudes intense, fresh flowery notes with a delicate fruity scent and hints of confectionery.

Liquor: The liquor exhibits a yellow/gold hue with shades of amber. It is slightly astringent on the palate, offering a rounded, long-lasting, velvety flavor. Fresh flowery top notes are followed by hints of ripe fruits, almonds, and spices.

Infusion: The infusion displays mixed colors, primarily brilliant green with brown and red tips. The flowery notes and nutty flavor linger in the mouth.

PREPARATION

For every 2/3 cup (150 milliliters) of water, use approximately 1/16 oz (2-3 grams) of tea leaves. Steep the tea at 185°F (85°C) for approximately 2-3 minutes.

Recommended with: Due to its tannin notes, this tea pairs perfectly with carbohydrates, savory quiches, eggs, cold cuts, lamb, game, marinated and smoked fish, as well as chocolate.

DARJEELING SEEYOK FTGFOP1 - FF

TYPE: BLACK TEA

AREA OF PROVENANCE: INDIA, DARJEELING, SEEYOK

Seeyok is known for producing organically grown first flush tea, located in the pristine Mirik Valley at an elevation ranging from 3,610 to 5,905 feet (1,100 to 1,800 meters) above sea level. Situated on the India-Nepal border, this area is protected by the Kanchenjunga mountain range, offering one of the most breathtaking Himalayan landscapes. Tea cultivation began here in 1869, and the plantations have recently shifted to organic farming methods, covering an area of over 370 acres (150 hectares).

Characterized by fog, cold mountain air, intermittent sunshine, and ample rainfall, this classic tea holds a Designation of Origin. Seeyok tea is best enjoyed during breakfast or in the afternoon, without the addition of milk, lemon, or sugar.

TASTING NOTES

Dry: The tea features large, very green leaves with hints of silver and hazelnut brown.

Liquor: The liquor has a golden-yellow hue, slightly astringent, and offers floral, vanilla, and almond notes typical of Darjeeling first flush teas, satisfying the senses.

Infusion: The steeped leaves are light green with hazelnut brown tips, emitting an even more intense fragrance of flowers with light empyreumatic (burnt or roasted) notes.

PREPARATION

For every 2/3 cup (150 milliliters) of water, use approximately 1/16 oz (2-3 grams) of tea leaves. Steep the tea at 185°F (85°C) for approximately 2-3 minutes.

Recommended with: tThanks to its elegant tannic notes, this tea pairs perfectly with a continental breakfast, carbohydrates, quiche, salmon, lamb, and chocolate.

BLACK TEA

ASSAM HATTIALLI FTGFOP1 - SF

TYPE: BLACK TEA

AREA OF PROVENANCE: INDIA, ASSAM, HATTIALLI

The name of this garden, Hattialli, means "road of the elephants." Positioned favorably and enjoying a pleasant climate, Hattialli can provide high-quality harvests throughout the year. This black Indian tea offers a rich, full-bodied taste, making it an excellent morning tea and a delightful choice with a touch of milk.

TASTING NOTES

Dry: The tea consists of regular, large leaves with a high proportion of golden shoots.

Liquor: The liquor is dark amber in color and full-bodied, striking a perfect balance between aromatic spiciness, maltiness, fruitiness, and cocoa notes. It offers a full-bodied, lingering flavor, making it undoubtedly the finest tea from Assam.

Infusion: The color of the infusion ranges between dark green, red, and brown.

PREPARATION

For every 2/3 cup (150 milliliters) of water, use approximately 1/16 oz (2-3 grams) of tea leaves. Steep the tea at 195°F (90°C) for approximately 3 minutes.

Recommended with: This tea pairs ideally with a continental or English breakfast, roast meats, and mushrooms.

ASSAM BANASPATY FTGFOP1 - FF

TYPE: BLACK TEA

AREA OF PROVENANCE: INDIA, ASSAM, BANASPATY

Teas from the Banaspaty gardens deliver everything you would expect from a high-quality Assam tea: it's a robust tea that's perfect for breakfast, renowned for its characteristic malty aroma. The first harvest yields a rich taste and a full-bodied aroma. First flush Assam teas, despite their quality, are relatively lesser-known in Europe. In contrast, second flush varieties are more commonly encountered and are frequently used in blending, including as an ingredient in Earl Grey blends.

TASTING NOTES

Leaf: The tea features regular dark brown leaves with golden shoots.
Liquor: The liquor has an amber color and entices the palate with slightly spicy notes and a malty, woody aroma. It offers a full-bodied, lingering flavor.
Infusion: The steeped leaves are dark and carry aromatic notes of fruitiness, woodiness, and maltiness.

PREPARATION

For every 2/3 cup (150 milliliters) of water, use approximately 1/16 oz (2-3 grams) of tea leaves. Steep the tea at 195°F (90°C) for approximately 3 minutes.

Recommended with: The malty notes of this tea pair gently with salmon. It is also delicious with a continental breakfast, red meats, and dark chocolate.

BLACK TEA

Indian Assam black tea, with its characteristic malty flavour and amber colour, is the breakfast tea par excellence.

NUWARA ELIYA HIGH GROWN

TYPE: BLACK TEA

AREA OF PROVENANCE: SRI LANKA, NUWARA ELIYA

Nuwara Eliya High Grown teas, cultivated at elevations ranging from 3,937 to 5,905 feet (1,200 to 1,800 meters) in the Nuwara Eliya region of Sri Lanka, are known for their delicate nature and can be likened to French Champagne in terms of their reputation. The high altitudes and consistently cold climate contribute to the slow growth of tea plants, resulting in unusually small leaves that take on an orange hue after drying. Another unique aspect of their taste comes from the wild mint, eucalyptus, and cypress that grow alongside the plantation.

TASTING NOTES

Dry: The leaves are of average size, occasionally featuring longer ones, and sometimes displaying a greenish color, which is unusual for this region.

Liquor: The liquor has a golden-orange color, slightly paler than other Sri Lankan tea varieties. It is light, delicate, yet characterized by a distinct personality. This tea can also be enjoyed iced during the summer months.

Infusion: The steeped leaves tend towards a coppery hue with dark green undertones.

PREPARATION

For every 2/3 cup (150 milliliters) of water, use approximately 1/16 oz (2-3 grams) of tea leaves. Brew the tea at 195-205°F (90-95°C) for around 3 minutes.

Recommended with: Nuwara Eliya High Grown tea complements a continental breakfast (bread, jam, cheese), an English breakfast (fried eggs, bacon, fried bread), lightly salted foods, cheeses (e.g., Provolone), and honey sweets.

BLACK TEA

RUHUNA GOLDEN TIPS

TYPE: BLACK TEA

AREA OF PROVENANCE: SRI LANKA, RUHUNA, MATARA DISTRICT

Ruhuna Golden Tips tea derives its name from the ancient Ceylonese term for the southern region of Sri Lanka and is considered the pearl of the island's teas. These "low-grown" teas are cultivated at altitudes ranging from 1,970 feet (600 meters) to sea level. Ruhuna Golden Tips tea is crafted exclusively from carefully selected long golden shoots. It is produced in very limited quantities and is renowned for its exceptional quality. Unlike other black teas, Golden Tips undergoes only slight oxidation. This tea originates from particularly fertile plantations near the Sinharaja rainforest, where the combination of humidity, rainfall, and unique soil bestows Golden Tips with an extraordinary and distinct aroma.

TASTING NOTES

Dry: The tea features long golden shoots covered with a soft down.

Liquor: The liquor has an amber-orange color and exudes a fresh, delicate scent with notes of flowers, fruit, and honey.

Infusion: The steeped leaves display a perfectly regular hazelnut color, accompanied by lingering flowery notes, hints of leather, and a spicy top note.

PREPARATION

For every 2/3 cup (150 milliliters) of water, use approximately 1/8 oz (3-5 grams) of tea leaves. Brew the tea at 195°F (90°C) for approximately 3 minutes.

Recommended with: Ruhuna Golden Tips pairs perfectly with a continental breakfast, lightly salted foods, mushrooms, vegetables, fish, and fruit pies.

UVA HIGH GROWN

TYPE: BLACK TEA

AREA OF PROVENANCE: SRI LANKA, UVA

Uva High Grown tea is one of the teas produced in the Uva region, located to the east of Nuwara Eliya and Dimbula on the central plateau of Sri Lanka. This tea is grown at an altitude of over 3,937 feet (1,200 meters). Its unique character is attributed to the local climate, which is influenced by several factors. The region is exposed to winds from both the north-east and the south-west, and despite experiencing monsoons, the climate remains relatively dry. This dryness is due to the surrounding mountains, which have numerous clefts that channel monsoon rains away from the tea plantations. The "dry" monsoons interrupt the normal process of photosynthesis in tea plants, and the combination of very hot days and cold nights results in chemical changes that enhance the tea's flavor.

TASTING NOTES

Dry: The tea features fairly long, curly leaves that are nearly black, occasionally with spots of brown.
Liquor: The liquor has a dark brown color and offers a sweet tea with an astringent, slightly minty taste, along with exotic notes of wood and spices. It is often used in blends and is best enjoyed without any additives.
Infusion: The steeped leaves tend towards a coppery hue.

PREPARATION

For every 2/3 cup (150 milliliters) of water, use approximately 1/16 oz (2-3 grams) of tea leaves. Brew the tea at 195-205°F (90-95°C) for approximately 3 minutes.

Recommended with: Uva High Grown tea complements a continental breakfast (bread, jam, cheese), an English breakfast (fried tomatoes, fried bread, eggs, bacon), mushroom risotto, couscous made with vegetables and white meats, pizza, salamis, and capers.

Though not widely drunk in the West, fermented teas are garnering more and more attention due to their precious properties.

FERMENTED (OR BLACK) TEA

The most famous black tea is Pu'er, a term that refers to a vast family of teas, including several loose-leaf and compressed varieties. The latter are shaped into bricks, cakes, nests, or melons. This tea is produced using a wide-leaf botanical specimen known as Da Ye, which grows in the southern part of Yunnan, on the border with Laos and Myanmar. Furthermore, to be classified as Pu'er, the leaves must have been sun-dried and undergone either natural or controlled fermentation. While Pu'er is currently categorized as a black tea, Chinese experts have recently debated whether to create a new tea category for it or keep it within the broader family of fermented teas produced both inside and outside Yunnan.

Chinese black teas are produced in regions such as Yunnan, Hunan, Sichuan, Hubei, and Guangxi. Chinese black tea is also referred to as Bianxiao Cha or "border-sale tea" because it was primarily consumed by frontier populations. Due to the challenging terrain in these mountainous regions, tea was historically transported on horseback to Tibet, Hong Kong, and Macao. For years, the Tea-Horse Road facilitated cultural exchange among different groups, nationalities, and religions, spreading the tea tradition worldwide.

The leaves of this type of tea undergo a true fermentation process. From a chemical standpoint, fermentation differs significantly from oxidation, as it is driven by microorganisms present on the tea leaves rather than exposure to oxygen. These are the only teas that are fermented and require seasoning before being sold, as only time can enhance their characteristic aroma. Moreover, the most valuable varieties are not consumed immediately but are set aside for aging.

The processing procedure begins by heating the tea leaves at high temperatures to halt oxidation and enzyme activity. Next, the leaves are rolled to release their essential oils and give them their shape. Subsequently, the leaves are sun-dried until they lose 90% of their water content. At this point, they are ready to be stacked in regular piles and sprayed with water, triggering the natural fermentation process. During the final drying stage, the leaves are scattered to air dry, eliminating any remaining moisture.

The medicinal properties of these teas have been valued in China since the Tang era. Since the 1970s, many Western scientific studies have also recognized their ability to aid digestion, significantly reduce levels of bad cholesterol in the blood, and lower the absorption of fat and sugar. This makes these teas valuable allies in weight management. Essentially, drinking three cups of fermented tea a day is akin to treating yourself to sips of health.

This spoutless teapot, in porcelain with blue decorations, enables the infusion to be repeated up to 10-12 times, and enhances the undergrowth aroma typical of Pu'er black. teas.

HOW TO PREPARE FERMENTED TEA

To prepare fermented Chinese teas, we recommend using a white porcelain or Yi Xing terracotta teapot. In China, there are sets designed for this purpose, typically made of white or decorated porcelain. These sets consist of a spoutless teapot and teacups with a wider diameter compared to those used for other types of tea.

To correctly prepare fermented tea, we suggest following these instructions:
1. Place the teapot, jug, and teacups on a ceremonial table with a special tray to catch any liquids.
2. Heat the water to 205°F (95°C), then pour it into the teapot, jug, and teacups to warm and rinse the tea set.
3. Empty the water and place tea leaves into the teapot (approximately 5-6 grams for every 2/3 of a cup or 150 ml). If the tea is in a compressed form, use a special knife to remove the desired quantity from the brick. It's preferable to infuse smaller pieces, as overly large and compact portions from a Pu'er cake may not yield an ideal infusion.
4. Pour hot water over the leaves or the portion of compressed brick, and give the tea a brief rinse.
5. Discard the rinse water and start the infusion. After about 1 minute, stop the infusion by pouring all of the tea into the jug, then serve it in the teacups.

When using the Chinese Gong Fu Cha method, fermented black teas can withstand around 10-12 infusions, each lasting approximately 1 minute.

If you prefer the European preparation method, you can perform a single infusion for 4-5 minutes using a quantity of 2-3 grams of tea leaves for every 2/3 of a cup (150 ml).

177

Pu'er black tea "cake." The portion of leaves required for the infusion is cut off horizontally, to avoid crushing the tea leaves, using a special knife for cutting compressed teas.

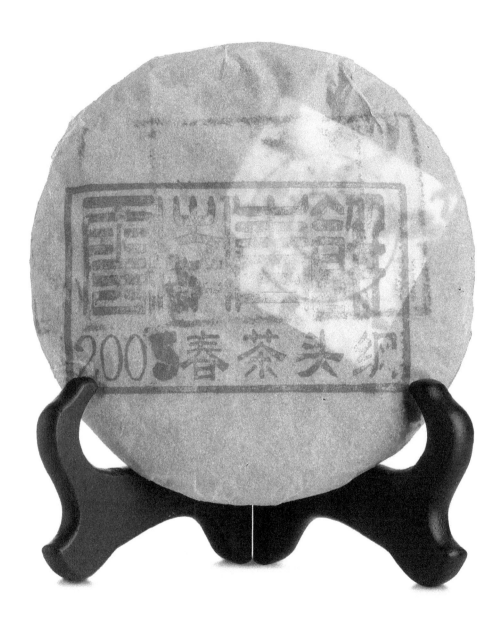

PU'ER SHENG CHA - CAKE

TYPE: FERMENTED TEA

AREA OF PROVENANCE: CHINA, YUNNAN, LIN CANG

Pu'er green tea (referred to as raw or "not cooked" tea) initially undergoes a processing procedure similar to that used for green teas. After harvesting, Pu'er leaves are traditionally sun-dried, which is one of the characteristics that make the processing of these teas unique.

If weather conditions are unfavorable or if quicker drying is required, the leaves are placed in ovens. However, it's worth noting that this can affect the tea's quality. Given the growing popularity of Pu'er teas, producers may be tempted to expedite the process using artificial methods, so careful attention is necessary. In the traditional process, ovens are only used to heat the cakes after the leaves have been compressed, primarily to remove residual moisture and prevent mold formation. The end result is an aromatic, complex liquor.

Aside from the cake shape, Pu'er Sheng Cha teas can also be found in various sizes and forms, such as small nests (tuo cha or mini tuo cha), square or rectangular bricks, melon shapes, or loose tea leaves.

Fresh Sheng Cha cakes can have an astringent taste with a slightly bitter note. They are initially fresh with a lingering flavor, and this tea undergoes a "refinement" phase over time. As time passes, the taste improves, and the tea releases more complex aromatic notes. Sampling it over time can be a fascinating experience. Once matured, the quality of Sheng Cha Pu'er teas often surpasses that of Shu Cha Pu'er teas.

TASTING NOTES

Dry: The tea cakes are gray-green in color, with visible shoots on the surface.
Liquor: A dull dark yellow; the taste is slightly bitter and herbal, sometimes with animal notes that dissipate during the natural aging process.
Infusion: The leaves turn khaki green.

PREPARATION

Western method: Use approximately 1/16 oz (2-3 grams) for every 2/3 cup (150 milliliters) of water at 205°F (95°C) for a 4-minute infusion.
Eastern method: Employ 1/8 oz (5 grams) for every 2/3 cup (150 milliliters) of water at 205°F (95°C). You can prepare up to 10 infusions, each lasting 1 minute, preceded by a quick rinse of the leaves.

Recommended with: Ideal with first-course vegetable-based dishes and fish-based second courses.

FERMENTED OR BLACK TEA

PU'ER SHU CHA - CAKE

TYPE: FERMENTED TEA

AREA OF PROVENANCE: CHINA, YUNNAN, LINCANG

Red Pu'er tea (known as cooked) undergoes a processing procedure similar to that used for green Pu'er Sheng Cha teas, along with a secret post-fermentation process. This process speeds up the aging and imparts the flavor of an aged Sheng Cha tea.

During this second fermentation, the leaves are placed under special impermeable sheets for 40-60 days.

Unlike green Pu'er Sheng Cha, which improves with age, Pu'er Shu Cha can be enjoyed immediately. These teas are a relatively recent innovation, introduced in the early 1970s to meet growing demand. This period marked a clear distinction in the history of fermented teas. All Pu'er teas processed before this date were authentic and fermented naturally, without any need for the chemical reactions introduced by humans.

TASTING NOTES

Dry: The cakes have a chocolate color with slightly lighter golden shoots on the surface.
Liquor: Very dark amber, brilliant, and crystal clear; the scent is reminiscent of wood, mushrooms, and forest earth. The sweet, delicate, and delicious flavor lingers persistently on the palate.
Infusion: Black leaves with intense notes of musk, wet earth, and wood.

PREPARATION

Western method: Use approximately 1/16 oz (2-3 grams) for every 2/3 cup (150 milliliters) of water at 205°F (95°C) for a 4-minute infusion.
Eastern method: Employ 1/8 oz (5 grams) for every 2/3 cup (150 milliliters) of water at 205°F (95°C). You can prepare up to 10-12 infusions, each lasting 1 minute, preceded by a quick rinse of the leaves.

Recommended with: Great with eggs, seasoned cheeses, red meats, cold cuts, and mushrooms.

PU'ER STEMS - BRICK

TYPE: FERMENTED TEA

AREA OF PROVENANCE: CHINA, YUNNAN, SIMAO

This highly unique compressed, fermented Pu'er tea is a specialty of Simao, one of the oldest tea-producing regions in Chinese history. Amongst the mountains in the far south of Yunnan, ancient wild tea plants with long stems flourish. This exceptional black tea is crafted from their tender branches. Unlike the leaves, it's the branches of the plant that are richest in amino acids, crucial for cell renovation. Much softer and more delicate than other Pu'er teas, this variety is recommended for those who wish to savor the forest scents characteristic of this tea family. With its remarkably low tannin content, this tea is suitable for any time of day.

TASTING NOTES

Dry: The tea brick made from branches is chocolate in color.
Liquor: Very dark amber, nearly black; the aroma evokes wood and damp forest earth. It is soft, delicate, and delightful on the palate.
Infusion: Black leaves with an intense scent of musk, damp earth, and wood.

PREPARATION

Western method: Use approximately 1/16 oz (2-3 grams) for every 2/3 cup (150 milliliters) of water at 205°F (95°C) for a 4-minute infusion.
Eastern method: Employ 1/8 oz (5 grams) for every 2/3 cup (150 milliliters) of water at 205°F (95°C). You can prepare up to 10-12 infusions, each lasting 1 minute, preceded by a quick rinse of the leaves.

Recommended with: Great with eggs, seasoned cheeses, red meats, cold cuts, and mushrooms.

FERMENTED OR BLACK TEA

FU CHA TOP GRADE - BRICK

TYPE: FERMENTED TEA

AREA OF PROVENANCE: CHINA, HUNAN, AN HUA

Hunan black tea, a classic and one of the most well-known Chinese black teas, has been utilized for centuries in traditional Chinese medicine. It has been used to address digestive issues, aid in weight loss diets, exhibit anti-arrhythmic effects on the heart, reduce cholesterol, and provide antibacterial properties. Fermented Fu Cha tea is rich in intestinal flora, acting as a natural antibiotic in the body. While it may not be widely recognized in the West, it plays a crucial role in the high-protein diets of Tibet, Mongolia, and the Northwest of China. It is an excellent source of minerals and vitamins, effective in regulating blood sugar and fat levels. Its nutritional properties can supplement diets lacking in fruits and vegetables. Originally called Hu Cha, it was renamed Fu Cha as this tea is compressed during the period known as Fu, or the hottest days of summer. It differs from Pu'er in that during the second phase of fermentation, a beneficial fungus known as "Golden Flower" (Eurotium Cristatum) forms. The quantity of fungus impacts Fu Cha's quality, with higher-quality samples containing more fungus.

TASTING NOTES

Dry: Very dark leaves compressed into bricks.
Liquor: Orange-amber, sweet and non-astringent, with aromatic flowery and woody notes. With high-quality samples, the taste lingers persistently on the palate.
Infusion: Very dark anthracite grey leaves tending towards black.

PREPARATION

Eastern method: Use 1/8 oz (5 grams) for every 2/3 cup (150 milliliters) of water at 205°F (95°C). Prepare up to 10-12 infusions, each lasting 60 seconds, preceded by a quick rinse of the leaves.

Recommended with: Ideal with pulse soups, red meats, seasoned cheeses, or after meals to aid digestion.

PROCESSED TEAS

SCENTED, FLAVORED, AND BLOOMING TEAS

As discussed earlier, Chinese teas are categorized into six macro-families based on their color classification, which depends on how the tea leaves are processed after harvesting.

Once the initial processing, unique to each tea category, is completed, the finished or "pure" product is ready for sale. However, in some instances, these teas can undergo further treatment to create what is known as "processed teas."

This macro-category encompasses scented, flavored, and blooming teas.

The art of "scenting" and "flavoring" tea leaves is an ancient Chinese tradition applied to various types of "pure" tea. Scented tea is primarily produced in the regions of Guangxi, Fujian, Sichuan, and Yunnan.

In scented teas, processed tea leaves come into contact with fresh flowers, such as jasmine, gardenia, orange blossom, sweet osmanthus, and roses.

After the flowers have imparted their delicate scent to the tea leaves, they are removed. Some flowers are left behind for aesthetic reasons even after the scenting process is complete.

Naturally, scented teas are much more delicate than flavored teas. Flavored teas achieve their aroma not through contact with fresh flowers but by adding natural or artificial flavorings that evoke the essence of flowers, fruits, spices, and more.

Blooming teas also fall within the macro-category of processed "pure" teas. In this case, tea shoots and flowers are intricately tied together in striking bundles, taking forms like spheres, mushrooms, towers, and even Buddhas. These teas infuse the liquor with a delicate floral aroma while delivering a visually stunning experience.

Considered meditation teas, these elegant "blooming teas" provide a captivating spectacle as they unfurl, making them a delightful treat not just for the palate but also for the eyes.

When brewed in a transparent cup, one can fully appreciate the enchanting transformation of the concealed flowers within these blooming teas.

20 RECIPES

BY CHEF GIOVANNI RUGGIERI

TEA TIME
AND SERVING
SUGGESTIONS

Tea ranks as the second most popular beverage globally, right after water, and is enjoyed throughout the day. There isn't a specific time for tea, as it complements various occasions, offering opportunities to explore pairings with both sweet and savory foods.

Tea proves to be an excellent companion during meals, as it cleanses the palate and amplifies the flavors of the food. Part of this effect is due to its usual consumption at a hot temperature, which heightens our taste perception.

Pairing tea with food is primarily a matter of personal preference, and there are no strict rules in this regard. However, adhering to some fundamental guidelines can help create harmonious matches between the unique flavors of different foods and the most appropriate teas.

Experimentation and practice can lead to finding an ideal balance, resulting in delightful sensory experiences. The key is for the taste elements to complement each other rather than overpower or mask one another. The goal is to establish a delicate sensory equilibrium based on either similarity or contrast. While the latter can be more challenging, they also yield the most innovative and successful pairings. In such cases, the tea should create a palate experience distinct from that of the food: for instance, if the dish is rich and oily, the tea should be crisp and mildly astringent; sweet desserts can be balanced by full-bodied, slightly bitter teas; robust or smoky flavors can be paired with delicate teas. Additionally, when tea is used as an ingredient in a dish, it should be served hot alongside the meal. Sugar, honey, and creamy desserts often benefit from sweet teas featuring floral or fruity notes.

THE MOST COMMON PAIRINGS ARE:

- LIGHT SALTED FOOD: CHINESE GREEN TEAS, WULONG TEAS, INDIAN BLACK TEAS
- CARBOHYDRATES: INDIAN OR SRI LANKAN BLACK TEAS, WULONG TEAS, GREEN TEAS
- VEGETABLES: WULONG TEAS, CHINESE AND JAPANESE GREEN TEAS
- EGGS: FERMENTED TEAS, SMOKED TEAS
- FISH: CHINESE AND JAPANESE GREEN TEAS, WHITE TEAS
- MOLLUSKS: JAPANESE GREEN TEAS
- WHITE MEAT: CHINESE AND JAPANESE GREEN TEAS, WHITE TEAS, YELLOW TEAS,
- INDIAN BLACK TEAS
- RED MEAT: SMOKED TEAS, CHINESE RED TEAS, INDIAN BLACK TEAS
- SMOKED FLAVORS: INDIAN BLACK TEAS, WULONG TEAS
- SHELLFISH: BERGAMOT-FLAVORED WULONG TEAS, CHINESE GREEN TEAS
- FRESH CHEESE: CHINESE AND JAPANESE GREEN TEAS, JASMINE PEARL TEAS
- BLUE CHEESE: JASMINE PEARL TEAS, WHITE TEAS, CHINESE RED TEAS
- MATURE CHEESE: SMOKED TEAS
- SPICY FOOD: JASMINE PEARL GREEN TEAS, CHINESE GREEN TEAS, WULONG TEAS
- DARK CHOCOLATE: INDIAN BLACK TEAS, BERGAMOT WULONG TEAS
- MILK OR WHITE CHOCOLATE: WULONG TEAS
- MUSHROOMS: FERMENTED TEAS, INDIAN OR SRI LANKAN BLACK TEAS
- FRUIT: CHINESE GREEN TEAS, WULONG TEAS, INDIAN BLACK TEAS
- NUTS: YELLOW TEAS
- PASTRIES: INDIAN BLACK TEAS, YELLOW TEAS

RED SHRIMP CRUDO WITH MATCHA GREEN MAYONNAISE AND SPROUTS

4 SERVINGS

FOR THE SHRIMP

12 SICILIAN RED SHRIMP, HEADS AND SHELLS REMOVED
OIL, AS NEEDED
SALT FLAKES, AS NEEDED
A FEW DROPS OF LEMON JUICE

FOR THE MAYONNAISE

1 EGG YOLK
1/16 OZ (2 G) SALT
10 DROPS LEMON JUICE
2/3 CUP (150 ML) EXTRA VIRGIN OLIVE OIL
1/4 OZ (10 G) MATCHA

FOR PLATING

SOME RADISH, TURNIP, AND GREEN SHISO SPROUTS
A FEW EDIBLE GERBER DAISY PETALS

PREPARATION

Freeze the shrimp for 12 hours. Once they have been defrosted (it is important that they are defrosted at room temperature), season them with a bit of oil, salt flakes, and a few drops of lemon juice.

To prepare the mayonnaise, beat the egg yolk with the salt and lemon juice. Once the components are well blended, add the extra virgin olive oil in a stream so that you obtain a thick mayonnaise. Lastly, add the matcha and gently stir.

To avoid that the sprouts and flower petals for garnish become withered, keep them in the refrigerator wrapped in a paper towel dampened with water so that they stay full and crispy until the dish is eaten.

JERUSALEM ARTICHOKE CREAM WITH POWDERED GOLDEN YUNNAN TEA, LIQUORICE, GREEN OIL AND KAMUT CRISP

4 SERVINGS

FOR THE JERUSALEM ARTICHOKE CREAM
14 OZ (400 G) JERUSALEM ARTICHOKES
2 TSP (10 ML) EXTRA VIRGIN OLIVE OIL
1/8 OZ (6 G) SALT
APPROX. 3/4 CUP (200 ML) FRESH CREAM
3 TBSP (50 ML) WATER

FOR THE GREEN OIL FOR THE KAMUT CRISP
7 OZ (200 G) PARSLEY
1 CUP (250 ML) EXTRA VIRGIN OLIVE OIL
APPROX 1/2 CUP (50 G) KAMUT FLOUR
1 3/4 OZ (50 G) BUTTER
1 3/4 OZ (50 G) EGG WHITES
APPROX. 1/8 OZ (7 G) SALT
APPROX. 1/16 OZ (3 G) BERGAMOT WULONG POWDER
APPROX. 1/4 OZ (8 G) GRATED LIQUORICE ROOT
APPROX. 1/4 OZ (8 G) GROUND GOLDEN YUNNAN TEA
A FEW RADISH SPROUTS
A FEW EDIBLE GERBER DAISY PETALS

PREPARATION

To prepare the cream, peel and cut the Jerusalem artichokes into small chunks, then brown them in a pot on high heat with extra virgin olive oil for 2 minutes. Salt, then add the cream and water. Reduce the heat to low and braise for 20 minutes, covering the pot with a lid. When the artichokes are cooked, puree them with a hand blender until you obtain a thick cream. If it is too dense, add a bit of water.

For the green oil, blanch the parsley (previously stripped from the stem) for 20 seconds, then cool it in ice water. Drain and squeeze out the excess water and blend in a blender for 10 minutes with the extra virgin olive oil until you obtain a dark green oil. Pour the parsley oil through cheesecloth to filter the chlorophyll.

To prepare the crisp, stir together all of the ingredients until you have obtained a homogeneous mixture. Using a small spoon, transfer the mixture onto a sheet of baking paper and spread it into strips, then bake at a temperature of 355 °F (180 °C) for 6 minutes.

To assemble the dish, first lay down the cream, then the sprouts and flower petals (which should always be one of the last elements of plating), the crisp, the liquorice, and tea powders, and lastly, the green oil. As liquorice has a strong aftertaste, sprinkle it on the Jerusalem artichoke cream in moderation using your thumb and index finger to create a stripe over the mixture. Do the same with the Golden Yunnan powder.

HERB SALAD WITH EDIBLE FLOWERS AND BLACK PU'ER TEA RICE CHIPS

4 SERVINGS

FOR THE BLACK PU'ER TEA RICE CHIPS
8 3/4 OZ (250 G) CARNAROLI RICE
OLIVE OIL AS NEEDED
1/2 OZ (14 G) BLACK PU'ER TEA LEAVES
OIL FOR FRYING AS NEEDED.

FOR THE SALAD
1 SMALL HEAD OF LOLLO ROSSO LETTUCE
1 SMALL HEAD OF DELICATE CURLY GREEN LETTUCE
1 SMALL HEAD OF LATE-SEASON RADICCHIO
1 SMALL HEAD OF GREEN GENTILINA LETTUCE
1 SMALL HEAD OF ENDIVE
1 HEAD OF ESCAROLE
CHERVIL AS NEEDED
SOME RED RADISH, DAIKON, SUNFLOWER, ONION, AND GREEN SHISO SPROUTS
SOME ROSE, VIOLET, AND EDIBLE GERBER DAISY PETALS

To prepare the chips, toast the rice with a bit of olive oil until the kernels are well toasted and hot. Then add enough slightly salted water to cover completely. Let it overcook, proceeding as you would for a risotto. Ten minutes before the rice is cooked, add the black Pu'er tea, and then finish cooking. The risotto must cook for around 40 minutes and be sufficiently creamy and thick. Be careful that it is not too wet. Then blend the rice in a food processor until it is creamy and smooth, free of lumps. Spread the mixture you have made on a silicone baking mat, creating strips that are well separated and not too thin. Let them dry thoroughly until they are crunchy, then let them puff up for a few moments in the heated frying oil and drain immediately.

Prepare the salad by combining all the ingredients. It is important to dress the salad at the last moment so that it is crunchy. Toss it gently to avoid damaging the leaves, and then let them gently fall onto the plate to remain fluffy.

STEAMED VEGETABLES WITH JASMINE SCENTED GREEN TEA POTATO CREAM

4 SERVINGS

FOR THE VEGETABLES

16 SMALL PINK TURNIPS

8 LEAVES TUSCAN CABBAGE

1 HEAD LATE-SEASON RADICCHIO, DIVIDED IN 4

1 HEAD ENDIVE, DIVIDED IN 4

1 SMALL HEAD OF CHARD

8 SMALL BUNCHES OF SPINACH

4 RADISHES

4 LEAVES OF SAVOY CABBAGE

EXTRA VIRGIN OLIVE OIL AS NEEDED

SALT AS NEEDED TO SALT THE VEGETABLES AFTER COOKING

FOR THE POTATO CREAM

1 LB 2 OZ (500 G) POTATOES

1 1/4 CUP (350 ML) FRESH CREAM

APPROX 1/8 OZ (6 G) SALT

1/2 OZ (16 G) JASMINE PEARL TEA

PREPARATION

Clean and cut the vegetables, then steam them separately. After cooking each of them for several minutes, arrange them on a tray covered with paper towels to eliminate any excess water. Dress with extra virgin olive oil and salt.

To prepare the cream, boil the potatoes in a tall saucepan for 45 minutes, then peel and place them in a blender. Add the cream, salt, and Jasmine Pearl tea. Blend for a few minutes until the tea has fully infused its flavor.

When plating, start by laying down the cream first. Use a serving spoon to spread it into stripes, on top of which you will arrange the blanched vegetables. It's important to dress them generously with extra virgin olive oil to make them more appetizing and glossy.

RICOTTA, SHRIMP AND BERGAMOT TEA

4 SERVINGS

8 FRESH SHRIMP
1/2 OZ (15 G) BERGAMOT WULONG TEA
1 2/3 CUP (400 ML) WATER
14 OZ (400 G) FRESH COW'S MILK RICOTTA
APPROX. 1/8 OZ (6 G) TAPIOCA FLOUR

FOR PLATING
A FEW PEA AND DAIKON SPROUTS
CHERVIL AS NEEDED
A FEW YELLOW VIOLET PETALS

PREPARATION

Peel the shrimp and freeze them for 12 hours; they should be very fresh, preferably still alive. Prepare the Bergamot Wulong tea infusion using 1 2/3 cups (400 ml) of water and 1/4 oz (10 grams) of tea. Set aside the remaining 1/8 oz (5 grams) of tea in a small bowl. Stir the ricotta and flavor it with 2 tbsp (40 ml) of the infusion and the remaining 1/8 oz (5 grams) of powdered tea. Cook the defrosted shrimp in the tea at a temperature of 80 °C (175 °F) for 2 minutes.

Boil the remaining tea for 10 minutes with the tapioca flour to reduce and condense it.

Now, for plating: start by dotting the ricotta on a soup plate. Next, add the cooled, thickened tea reduction, followed by the shrimp, and finally, garnish with chervil, flower petals, and sprouts.

WULONG SHUI XIAN RAVIOLI WITH RADISHES, TURNIP GREENS, AND BEET POWDER

4 SERVINGS

FOR THE PASTA

APPROX. 2 1/2 CUPS (300 G) TYPE 0 FLOUR
APPROX. 1 1/2 CUP (200 G) SEMOLINA FLOUR
APPROX. 12 1/2 OZ (375 G) EGG YOLKS

FOR THE WULONG SHUI XIAN RAVIOLI FILLING

14 OZ (400 G) RICOTTA
APPROX. 1/4 OZ (12 G) WULONG SHUI XIAN TEA, GROUND WELL
APPROX. 1/16 OZ (3 G) SALT
1/16 OZ (2 G) FRESHLY GROUND BLACK PEPPER

FOR THE SAUCE

1 1/3 LBS (600 G) SMALL LEAF TURNIP GREENS
8 GREEN LEAF RADISHES
1/4 OZ (10 G) WULONG SHUI XIAN TEA POWDER
3 1/2 OZ (100 G) BUTTER

PREPARATION

For the pasta, thoroughly combine the flours and egg yolks until the dough becomes uniform and dense.

Season the ricotta filling with Wulong Shui Xian tea powder, salt, and pepper.

To make the ravioli, roll out the pasta dough to a thickness of approximately 1 millimeter. Then, cut the dough into 2 x 2 inch (5 x 5 cm) squares. Place a portion of the filling in the center of each square, fold it over to create a triangle, and seal it to form the classic ravioli shape.

Clean the turnip greens and radishes, and briefly blanch them in salted water for no more than 2 minutes. Melt the butter, sprinkle the ravioli with Wulong Shui Xian powder, and add some melted butter to enhance the flavor. Combine the ravioli, turnip greens, and radishes in the melted butter off the heat. Then, plate the dish in a large soup bowl.

TEA TIME AND SERVING SUGGESTIONS

JAPANESE GENMAICHA TEA SOUP WITH VEGETABLES, SPROUTS, AND FLOWER PETALS

4 SERVINGS

FOR THE SOUP

APPROX. 3 1/2 CUPS (800 ML) WATER
APPROX. 3/4 OZ (22 G) GENMAICHA TEA
8 BABY CARROTS, GREENS LEFT ON
8 PURPLE TURNIPS
3 1/2 OZ (100 G) CELERY
8 SMALL FENNEL BULBS
5 OZ (150 G) SAVOY CABBAGE
APPROX. 1/4 OZ (8 G) SALT

FOR PLATING

8 3/4 OZ (250 G) WHEAT SPROUTS
A FEW RED ROSE PETALS
A FEW GARLIC AND SUNFLOWER SPROUTS
2 1/2 OZ (70 G) PEA SPROUTS

PREPARATION

Prepare a Genmaicha infusion using the specified amount of water and tea. After 5 minutes, strain it through a fine mesh sieve.

Clean the baby carrots, turnips, celery, fennel, and cabbage. Chop the vegetables into pieces of similar size and boil them for 2 minutes in salted water.

Once that is done, pour the Genmaicha infusion into a soup bowl and add the vegetables. Finally, combine the wheat sprouts, flower petals, and the other sprouts. To maintain the crunchiness of the vegetables and sprouts, quickly arrange all the components on the plate and serve the soup very hot.

TEA TIME AND SERVING SUGGESTIONS

SENCHA AND RED RADISH SPROUT RISOTTO

4 SERVINGS

FOR THE RISOTTO

APPROX. 2 TBSP (25 ML) EXTRA VIRGIN OLIVE OIL
12 1/2 OZ (350 G) VIALONE NANO RICE
APPROX. 1/2 CUP (100 ML) WHITE WINE
1/4 OZ (10.5 G) SENCHA TEA
1 OZ (30 G) BUTTER FOR MOUNTING THE RISOTTO
APPROX. 3 TBSP (50 ML) EXTRA VIRGIN OLIVE OIL
FOR MOUNTING THE RISOTTO
SALT AS NEEDED
A FEW RED RADISH SPROUTS

PREPARATION

Bring a large quantity of salted water to a boil, which will be added to the rice to absorb. In a large saucepan, add the extra virgin olive oil and toast the rice, seasoning it slightly with salt, until the kernels are searing hot. Add the white wine and let it simmer. When it has completely evaporated, start adding the salted water, then incorporate the Sencha tea and continue cooking over high heat for 12 minutes.

At the end, the rice should be almost dry. At this point, add the butter and the extra virgin olive oil, add a ladle of the cooking water from the rice, and vigorously stir the risotto in the pan so that all of the starches in the rice are released. Adjust the salt and serve on a plate. When it is ready to serve, let the radish sprouts gently fall over the risotto so that they do not cook due to the heat.

LAPSANG SOUCHONG SPAGHETTI CARBONARA

4 SERVINGS

FOR THE SPAGHETTI

1 OZ (30 G) LAPSANG SOUCHONG
3 1/2 CUPS (600 G) SEMOLINA FLOUR
3/4 CUP (160 ML) WATER
7 OZ (200 G) EGG YOLKS
3 1/3 CUPS (300 G) PARMIGIANO REGGIANO CHEESE
1/2 OZ (15 G) FRESHLY GROUND BLACK PEPPER
APPROX. 1/4 OZ (8 G) SALT
4 CUPS (1 L) CREAM
POWDERED LAPSANG SOUCHONG AS NEEDED

PREPARATION

Grind the Lapsang Souchong tea and mix it with the semolina flour. Stir until the semolina flour is evenly speckled with black, then add the water and mix for 5 minutes. The dough should be very floury and grainy. Pass the dough through an extruder with a 0.01 (2 mm) bronze die, then place the spaghetti you have obtained in the refrigerator on a steel cookie sheet on top of a paper towel.

In the meantime, mix the egg yolks, Parmigiano Reggiano, salt, and pepper in a steel bowl. Place this mixture in a double boiler and add the cream. Bring the mixture up to a temperature of 180 °F (82 °C), continuously beating with a whisk to prevent the egg yolks from becoming lumpy.

Boil plenty of salted water for the spaghetti, then cook for 2 minutes over high heat and drain. Mix with the Parmigiano Reggiano cream away from the heat. Serve by sprinkling with a dash of powdered Lapsang Souchong.

FONDUE-STUFFED POTATO GNOCCHI IN BLACK DARJEELING TEA BROTH

4 SERVINGS

FOR THE FONDUE

7 OZ (200 G) FONTINA
3 EGG YOLKS
1 CUP (250 ML) WHOLE MILK

FOR THE GNOCCHI

4 1/2 LB (2 KG) YELLOW POTATOES
4 EGG YOLKS
APPROX. 3/4 CUP (70 G) PARMIGIANO
REGGIANO CHEESE, GRATED
1/4 OZ (9 G) SALT
APPROX. 2 1/2 CUPS (300 G) TYPE 0 FLOUR

FOR THE BLACK DARJEELING TEA BROTH

3/4 OZ (20 G) DARJEELING CASTLETON TEA
2 CUPS (500 ML) WATER

FOR PLATING

A FEW DAIKON SPROUTS

PREPARATION

Cut the fontina into pieces and place it in a double boiler. Then add the egg yolks and milk. Bring the mixture up to a temperature of 175 °F (80 °C). Afterward, mix it with a hand blender and use it to fill a pastry bag. Refrigerate for about 2 hours.

Cook the potatoes in salted water for around 45 minutes. Peel and mash them with a potato masher on a wooden cutting board. Let them cool. Add the egg yolks, Parmigiano Reggiano, salt, and flour. Knead quickly, without spending too much time on the dough (the more you knead it, the softer it will become). Stretch the dough between two sheets of baking paper to a maximum width of a quarter of an inch (0.5 cm). Then cut the dough into squares of around 1.5 inches (4 cm) per side. Fill the center of each square with the fondue and seal it as you would a dumpling.

Lastly, prepare the black Darjeeling tea broth by placing the indicated amount of tea to infuse in the water for 5 minutes and then straining it through a fine-mesh sieve.

Cook the gnocchi for 2-3 minutes, then serve them in a soup plate where you have already poured some of the hot Darjeeling broth. Finally, garnish with daikon sprouts and serve.

WULONG DONG DING LAMB WITH JERUSALEM ARTICHOKE CREAM

4 SERVINGS

FOR THE WULONG DONG DING TEA REDUCTION
1/2 OZ (14 G) WULONG DONG DING TEA
APPROX. 3/4 CUP (200 ML) WATER
APPROX. 1/4 OZ (8 G) TAPIOCA FLOUR

FOR THE VEGETABLES
4 SMALL HEADS OF CHARD
4 BABY FENNEL BULBS
EXTRA VIRGIN OLIVE OIL AS NEEDED
SALT AS NEEDED

FOR THE LAMB
2 SMALL RACKS OF LAMB, AROUND 12 1/2 OZ (350 G EACH)
EXTRA VIRGIN OLIVE OIL AS NEEDED
BUTTER AS NEEDED
SAGE, ROSEMARY, AND BAY LEAF AS NEEDED

FOR THE JERUSALEM ARTICHOKE CREAM
2 1/4 LB (1 KG) JERUSALEM ARTICHOKES
1 1/2 CUP (400 ML) FRESH CREAM

FOR PLATING
POWDERED WULONG DONG DING TEA AS NEEDED

PREPARATION

Prepare an infusion of Wulong Dong Ding by steeping the indicated amount of tea in water for 4 minutes, then filter it through a fine-mesh sieve. Add the tapioca flour and reduce for 20 minutes over very low heat. Fill a pastry bag with the reduction and let it cool for at least 4 hours.

Prepare the lamb by trimming any excess fat, then brown it in a nonstick pan with a bit of extra virgin olive oil, letting all sides brown. Add the butter and spices and reduce the flame to low. With the help of a spoon, continue to baste with the hot butter until it's cooked and pink in the center. Cut between the ribs to separate them and let the meat rest for a few minutes so that it loses any excess blood.

Boil the chard and the baby fennel, and garnish them with a bit of olive oil and salt.

Arrange a few drops of the tea reduction on the serving plate, and place the lamb, the chard, and the fennel on top. Sprinkle with a bit of Wulong Dong Ding tea and serve.

LONG JING POACHED PRAWNS WITH CRUNCHY VEGETABLES

4 SERVINGS

FOR THE VEGETABLES
3 ZUCCHINI
3 CARROTS
4 BABY FENNELS
2 CELERY STALKS

FOR THE PRAWNS
APPROX. 1/4 OZ (12 G) LONG JING TEA
APPROX. 1 13/4 CUP (400 ML) WATER
8 PRAWNS

FOR PLATING
CHERVIL AS NEEDED
A FEW PEA AND GREEN SHISO SPROUTS
A FEW EDIBLE GERBER DAISY PETALS
A FEW LONG JING TEA LEAVES

PREPARATION

Clean and wash the vegetables. Remove the white part of the zucchini, cutting them into four pieces lengthwise and then into small pieces diagonally. Cut the carrots and celery in the same way. Sauté the vegetables over high heat in a nonstick pan, then add a ladleful of water and let it evaporate.

In the meantime, prepare the tea infusion and let it steep for 3 minutes. Filter it once it is off the heat, and then immerse the previously shelled prawns in the tea for 4 minutes so that the flesh is tender and not affected by boiling.

Serve the prawns on a plate with the crunchy vegetables, the chervil, sprouts, flower petals, and a few Long Jing leaves.

LEG OF GUINEA FOWL WITH CARROT PUREE AND MOROCCAN MINT TEA

4 SERVINGS

FOR THE LEG OF GUINEA FOWL
1 3/4 OZ (50 G) CELERY
1 3/4 OZ (50 G) CARROTS
1 3/4 OZ (50 G) ONION
4 LEGS OF GUINEA FOWL
OIL, AS NEEDED
2/3 CUP (150 ML) WHITE WINE
1/4 OZ (10 G) TOMATO PASTE
SALT AND PEPPER AS NEEDED

FOR THE CARROT PUREE
14 OZ (400 G) CARROTS
APPROX. 1/2 CUP (100 ML)
EXTRA VIRGIN OLIVE OIL
SALT AS NEEDED

FOR THE MOROCCAN TEA REDUCTION
APPROX. 1/4 OZ (8 G) MINT GREEN TEA
APPROX. 3/4 CUP (200 ML) WATER
APPROX. 1/4 OZ (8 G) CASSAVA FLOUR

FOR PLATING
14 OZ (400 G) SPINACH LEAVES
A FEW FRESH MINT LEAVES
SALT AS NEEDED

PREPARATION

Dice the celery, carrot, and onion into small pieces, then brown them well with a bit of salt. Meanwhile, brown the guinea fowl on each side in a nonstick pan with a bit of olive oil until it is dark brown in color. Then, add the white wine and simmer until it boils. Add the tomato paste and pour all of this into the mirepoix of celery, carrots, and onion. Cook for around one and a half hours, adjusting the water if necessary, and season with salt and pepper.

While the guinea fowl is cooking, prepare the puree: peel and clean the carrots, then cut them into small pieces. Brown them in a bit of extra virgin olive oil and salt, then cover with a bit of water. Cook until the liquid is reduced by almost half, then blend with a beater, adding a bit more extra virgin olive oil and salt while mixing.

Prepare the Moroccan tea, let it cool and filter it, then add the cassava flour and reduce it over very low heat until the infusion acquires a gelatinous consistency.

Blanch some of the spinach for a few minutes in plenty of salted water, but do not overcook it; otherwise, the color and consistency of the spinach can be ruined from overcooking.

Once the one and a half hours of cooking time for the guinea fowl have passed, check that the meat is fully cooked and serve it with the carrot puree, Moroccan tea reduction, spinach, a few fresh mint leaves, and the guinea fowl cooking juices, filtered and reduced by boiling into a dense and flavorful gravy.

BATTERED FRIED SMELTS WITH SPROUTS AND OSMANTHUS WULONG REDUCTION

4 SERVINGS

1 1/3 LBS (600 G) SMELTS

FOR THE BATTER
3 1/2 OZ (100 G) CORN STARCH
APPROX. 2 1/2 CUPS (300 G) TYPE 0 FLOUR
1/8 OZ (5 G) YEAST
APPROX. 3/4 CUP (200 ML) SPARKLING WATER
4 CUPS (1 L) VEGETABLE OIL FOR FRYING

FOR THE OSMANTHUS WULONG TEA INFUSION
3/4 OZ (20 G) OSMANTHUS WULONG TEA
APPROX. 3/4 CUP (200 ML) WATER
APPROX. 1/4 OZ (8 G) CASSAVA FLOUR

FOR PLATING
CHERVIL AS NEEDED
A FEW CURLY OR LETTUCE SPROUTS
A FEW VIOLET PETALS

PREPARATION

Mix the cornstarch and the type 0 flour in a bowl. Add the yeast and the sparkling water and mix by hand until you obtain a soft and smooth batter. Place it in the coldest part of the fridge.

Put the frying oil in a suitable pan and heat it to a temperature of 350°F (180°C).
While the oil is heating, prepare the Osmanthus Wulong tea infusion. Then, add the cassava flour and bring it to a gentle boil for around 25 minutes until the tea thickens. Cool it and use it to fill a pastry bag.

At this point, get the smelts and the frying batter. Dip the smelts one by one into the batter and fry them individually to prevent them from sticking together while cooking.

Place a few drops of the tea on the serving plate using the pastry bag and place one fried fish on each drop of tea. Garnish with chervil, sprouts, and flower petals.

FRIED CHICKEN HEARTS WITH HUANG SHAN MAO FENG POACHED VEGETABLES AND BUCKWHEAT POLENTINA

4 SERVINGS

**FOR THE POLENTINA
(A THINNER VARIATION OF POLENTA)**

2 CUPS (500 ML) WATER
SALT AS NEEDED
7 OZ (200 G) "POLENTA TARAGNA" (FROM CORN AND BUCKWHEAT)

FOR THE VEGETABLES

14 OZ (400 G) CELERY
EXTRA VIRGIN OLIVE OIL AS NEEDED
SALT AS NEEDED
5 OZ (150 G) LATE-SEASON RADICCHIO

FOR THE CHICKEN

1 1/3 LBS (600 G) CHICKEN HEARTS
SALT, PEPPER, AND EXTRA VIRGIN OLIVE OIL AS NEEDED

FOR THE HUANG SHAN MAO FENG INFUSION

1/4 OZ (10 G) HUANG SHAN MAO FENG TEA
APPROX. 3/4 CUP (200 ML) WATER

PREPARATION

Boil the water in a small saucepan, lightly salting it, and sprinkle the polenta into the water, mixing constantly with a whisk. Cook for 45 minutes.

In the meantime, clean and wash the celery, then cut it diagonally into diamonds that are slightly less than one inch in diameter. Quickly sauté them in a bit of extra virgin olive oil, add salt, and then let them sizzle for around a minute. Add a bit of water to help with the cooking.

Clean and wash the radicchio, keeping only the ends of the innermost leaves.

Salt and pepper the chicken hearts and brown them in extra virgin olive oil over high heat, letting them color until dark brown. Then, add the Huang Shan Mao Feng tea and let it simmer and reduce until the sauce is thick, glossy, and dense.
Assemble everything on a serving plate and serve.

MATCHA TIRAMISU

4 SERVINGS

FOR THE SAVOIARDI COOKIES (LADYFINGERS)
4 EGGS
1 1/4 CUP (250 G) SUGAR
2 1/4 CUPS (280 G) TYPE 00 FLOUR
GRATED LEMON ZEST AS NEEDED

FOR SOAKING THE COOKIES
1 2/3 CUP (400 ML) WATER
14 OZ (400 G) SUGAR
APPROX. 3/4 OZ (18 G) POWDERED BANCHA TEA
1/8 OZ (5 G) WILDFLOWER HONEY

FOR THE MASCARPONE CREAM
1 CUP (200 G) SUGAR
8 EGG YOLKS
14 OZ (400 G) MASCARPONE CHEESE
3/4 OZ (20 G) MATCHA POWDER
7 OZ (200 G) LIGHTLY WHIPPED CREAM

PREPARATION

To prepare the cookies, beat the eggs with the sugar for 25 minutes with an electric mixer. When the mixture appears whipped and quite solid, sprinkle in the flour, folding very delicately with a spatula from bottom to top to prevent lumps from forming. Then, add a bit of grated lemon zest. Pour the mixture into a nonstick baking pan lined with paper and bake for 25 minutes at 350 °F (175 °C). When finished, wait a few minutes for the mixture to cool, then cut into uniform rectangles around 1 x 3 inches (2 x 6 cm) in size.

Prepare the liquid to dip the cookies by mixing all of the ingredients together, then quickly dip the cookies and arrange them into a tight and uniform layer in a baking pan.

In the meantime, for the cream, beat the sugar with the egg yolks until the mixture has puffed up, is light, and perfectly whipped. Add the mascarpone a little at a time, having previously whisked it, the matcha powder, and lastly, the lightly whipped cream, which you will finish whipping when you incorporate it into the mixture. Cut the savoiardi in the pan using a cookie cutter, and arrange the shaped pieces on plates. Finish the dessert by covering it with the mascarpone cream.

YOGURT BAVARIAN CREAM WITH VANILLA AND GREEN LYCHEE TEA SAUCE

4 SERVINGS

FOR THE CREAM
APPROX. 3/4 CUP (200 ML) WATER
1/2 CUP (100 G) SUGAR
1/4 OZ (10 G) GELATIN
JUICE OF HALF A LEMON
1 CUP (250 G) YOGURT
APPROX. 3/4 CUP (200 ML) FRESH
WHIPPING CREAM

FOR THE VANILLA AND GREEN LYCHEE TEA SAUCE
5 EGG YOLKS
1/4 CUP (50 G) SUGAR
1/8 OZ (5 G) VANILLA ESSENCE
2 CUPS (500 ML) MILK
3/4 OZ (20 G) GROUND GREEN LYCHEE TEA

FOR PLATING
CHERVIL AS NEEDED
A FEW RED ROSE PETALS
A FEW MINT SPROUTS

PREPARATION

For the Bavarian cream, boil the water and sugar, then add and melt the gelatin, which you have previously softened for a few minutes in cold water and squeezed out any excess water when removed from the heat. Mix well so that no solid residue of the gelatin remains. Add the lemon juice and yogurt, ensuring that the water, sugar, and gelatin syrup are not boiling but are instead at room temperature. Then, whip the cream and combine the two mixtures until you have obtained a smooth and well-blended cream. Pour the mixture into your molds of choice and place them in the refrigerator for at least 4 hours.

To prepare the sauce, blend the egg yolks, sugar, and vanilla well. Boil the milk, flavoring it with the Green Lychee tea powder, then add the egg and sugar mixture a little at a time, continuing to stir. Cook the mixture over a double boiler, bringing it to a temperature of 180 °F (82 °C), stirring continuously. Let cool quickly over water and ice, whisking continuously even after cooking to prevent lumps from forming.

Plate the dessert, decorating with chervil, flower petals, and sprouts.

WHITE CHOCOLATE COULIS WITH BERGAMOT TEA AND VIOLETS

4 SERVINGS

FOR THE COULIS
1 LB 2 OZ (500 G) WHITE CHOCOLATE
1 1/4 CUP (350 ML) MILK
2 3/4 OZ (80 G) SUGAR

FOR THE BERGAMOT TEA INFUSION
1/2 OZ (15 G) GROUND BERGAMOT WULONG TEA
APPROX. 1/2 CUP (100 ML) WATER

FOR PLATING
A FEW EDIBLE RED AND YELLOW VIOLET PETALS
A FEW MINT SPROUTS

PREPARATION

Melt the chocolate in a double boiler with the milk and sugar, bringing the temperature up to 120°F (50°C).

Prepare the Bergamot tea infusion and add it to the chocolate, filtering the mixture through a cloth.

Plate the chocolate coulis, and only then decorate with the flowers, mint sprouts, and powdered Bergamot Wulong tea.

It is important that the coulis does not exceed 120°F (50°C), as excessive heat may change the equilibrium of the chocolate.

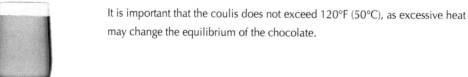

72% DARK CHOCOLATE MOUSSE WITH BLACK SALT FLAKES AND MOROCCAN MINT TEA HONEY

4 SERVINGS

FOR THE MOUSSE

8 3/4 OZ (250 G) 72% DARK CHOCOLATE
APPROX. 1 CUP (180 G) SUGAR
APPROX. 1/2 CUP (100 ML) WATER
APPROX. 1/4 OZ (12 G) GELATIN
APPROX. 2 1/2 CUP (600 ML) WHIPPING CREAM

FOR THE MOROCCAN MINT TEA REDUCTION

APPROX. 3/4 CUP (200 ML) WATER
APPROX. 1/4 OZ (8 G) MINT GREEN TEA
1/8 OZ (5 G) GELATIN

FOR PLATING

APPROX. 1/8 OZ (4 G) COARSE FLAKE SALT
A FEW VIOLET, RED ROSE, AND EDIBLE GERBER DAISY PETALS
CHERVIL AS NEEDED
A FEW MINT SPROUTS

PREPARATION

Melt the chocolate with the sugar in a double boiler along with the water and gelatin that you have previously softened in cold water and then squeezed out. Whip the cream and add it to the chocolate.

For the Moroccan mint tea reduction, boil the water and add the mint tea once the heat is off. Let steep for 6 minutes, then add the gelatin (previously softened in water and ice), and let solidify in the refrigerator for at least 3 hours. Using a pastry bag, decorate the plate with dots using the tea reduction before laying down the quenelles of chocolate mousse.

Let the mousse rest for at least 4 hours in the refrigerator. When it is quite cold, make four quenelles using a soup spoon and place one in the center of each plate, then arrange the flower petals as desired, along with the chervil and mint sprouts. Garnish with a few flakes of salt and serve.

WARM HAZELNUT MINI CAKES WITH HAZELNUT, AND GENMAICHA TEA CREAM

4 SERVINGS

FOR THE CAKES

7 EGGS
APPROX. 1 1/2 CUP (300 G) SUGAR
APPROX. 12 1/2 OZ (370 G) CHOPPED HAZELNUTS
APPROX. 1/4 OZ (8 G) GENMAICHA TEA
APPROX. 1/16 OZ (3 G) BAKING POWDER

FOR THE HAZELNUT CREAM

3 1/2 OZ (100 G) HAZELNUT PASTE
APPROX. 3 TBSP (50 ML) CREAM
1/4 CUP (50 G) SUGAR
1 OZ (30 G) CHOPPED HAZELNUTS

PREPARATION

To prepare the cakes, separate the egg yolks from the whites and beat the yolks with the sugar. Add the chopped hazelnuts and Genmaicha tea to the yolk and sugar mixture. Add the baking powder and then the whites, which have been beaten until stiff. Pour the mixture into individual greased molds and bake at 340 °F (170 °C) for 25 minutes.

For the hazelnut cream, combine all of the ingredients in a steel bowl and cook in a double boiler, bringing the temperature to 150 °F (65 °C) until all of the elements have thickened.

Here is a small tip to get the most intense flavor: serve the hazelnut cakes warm, if possible cooking them up to the last minute, so that all of the flavors can be clearly distinguished.

GLOSSARY

IN THIS SECTION, WE WILL PROVIDE A CONCISE GLOSSARY OF TERMS USED TO TASTE AND ASSESS THE QUALITY OF TEA.

PLEASE NOTE THAT THIS LIST IS NOT EXHAUSTIVE, AND IT MAY NOT ADHERE TO STRICT TECHNICAL ACCURACY. DIFFERENT CULTURES HAVE DEVELOPED THEIR OWN TEA TERMINOLOGY, AND EACH TEA TASTER AND EXPERT MAY HAVE THEIR UNIQUE CONTRIBUTIONS.

THE FOLLOWING OVERVIEW IS INTENDED AS A GENERAL INTRODUCTION TO CONVEY SOME OF THE INTRIGUING AND VIBRANT EXPRESSIONS ASSOCIATED WITH THE WORLD OF TEA.

COMMENTS ON THE APPEARANCE OF LEAVES

Body: Refers to the appearance of tea leaves, which can be categorized as old or tender, light or heavy, and with thick or thin flesh. Generally, tender, thick, and heavy leaves are considered higher quality.

Clear tip: White down on the tea shoot is known as "white tip." If there are several tips covered in thick down, they are referred to as "clear tips," which can be gold, silver, or grey.

Dry: Dry tea leaves that have not yet been steeped.

Flawed leaf: A tea leaf with rough edges due to poor cutting.

Heaviness: Rolled leaves that feel substantial in the hand.

Infusion: Steeped tea leaves removed from the water.

Powder: Finely ground tea, often associated with lower quality tea and used in tea bags.

Shoots: Tender tips covered with white down that have not fully grown into leaves.

Tender Tea consisting mainly of tender shoots with one or two leaves, characterized by their round, narrow, thin, and sharp-pointed tips.

Uneven leaves: Leaves that vary in shape or thickness.

Well proportioned leaves: Leaves with a uniform shape, regardless of size or weight.

COMMENTS ON THE COLOR OF LEAVES

Black-brown: Brownish black with shades of grey.

Brilliant: Leaves with a bright and vivid color.

Even: Leaves with a consistent and uniform color.

Green-black: Leaves that are both green and black, velvety, and evenly colored.

Grass green: Pale green, often associated with older or lower-quality leaves or insufficient enzyme blocking during processing.

Matt: Dull and lusterless leaves, typical of older leaves.

Mixed: Leaves with uneven coloration.

Rich green: Shiny jade-green leaves.

Rust: Dark and matte red leaves.

COMMENTS ON THE SCENT

Aroma: The overall scent perceived indirectly in the mouth.

Bouquet: The combination of fragrances detected in the nose.

Burnt: A scent resembling burning, often caused by inappropriate processing.

Delicate aroma: A refined and elegant scent without dominant notes.

Elegant aroma: A graceful and sophisticated floral scent with no specific flower dominating.

Grass aroma: The scent of grass and leaves.

Pure and semi-sweet: A balanced and slightly sweet aroma.

Sweet aroma: A scent reminiscent of honey, syrup, or lychees.

Toasted rice aroma: A popcorn-like aroma associated with lightly toasted teas.

Vegetable aroma: A fresh, vegetable-like scent, often used to describe green tea.

COMMENTS ON THE COLOR OF THE LIQUOR

- *Brilliant:* Clear and shiny liquid. Orange: Yellow with a hint of red, similar to the color of ripe oranges.
- *Brilliant green:* Bright green with hints of yellow, characteristic of high-quality green tea.
- *Cloudy:* Unclear liquor with suspended particles.
- *Golden:* Mainly yellow with shades of orange, bright like gold.
- *Green-yellow:* Green with a touch of yellow.
- *Light yellow:* Clear and light yellow.
- *Orange-red:* Dark yellow with reddish hues.
- *Liquor:* The liquid portion of the tea.
- *Red:* Overheated or aged liquor, with light or dark red tones.
- *Yellow-green:* Yellow with a hint of green.

COMMENTS ON THE TASTE OF THE LIQUOR

- *Astringent:* Causes a dry sensation in the mouth, often due to non-oxidized polyphenols (typical of green tea).
- *Bitter:* An intense, bitter, and slightly sour taste that may dull the taste buds.
- *Brisk:* A strong, invigorating, and refreshing flavor.
- *Crude and sour:* An underripe, strong, and sour taste, usually resulting from insufficient withering.
- *Crude and tasteless:* Insipid and tending toward bitterness.
- *Fresh:* A fresh and delightful taste, often slightly acidic, leaving a refreshing sensation.
- *Full-bodied:* A strong, robust flavor.
- *Generous:* Rich and dense, full-flavored without being overly sweet.
- *Grassy and sour:* A strong, sour, and grassy taste.
- *Malty:* A flavor reminiscent of malt, indicating good quality tea.
- *Metallic:* An unpleasant taste associated with poorly processed tea.
- *Persistent:* Leaves a lingering flavor in the mouth.
- *Pungent:* Astringent without being bitter.
- *Pure and delicate:* Ripe but not overly dense.
- *Refined:* A subtle and sophisticated taste and aroma.
- *Rounded:* Fills the mouth with a sense of fullness.
- *Semi-sweet:* Slightly sweet and balanced in aroma.
- *Smoked:* Tea dried over smoky flames, imparting a smoky aroma.
- *Strong:* A full, highly astringent taste, typical of dark liquors.
- *Subtle:* A flavor marked by delicate yet complex aromas.
- *Sweet:* Slightly sugary and non-astringent.
- *Tannic:* The flavor of teas rich in tannins or polyphenols.
- *Tasteless or flat:* Thin and insipid tea.
- *Umami:* One of the five basic flavors perceived by taste buds, often used in Asian cuisine to describe the taste of glutamates found in certain Japanese green teas.
- *Velvety:* A harmonious flavor reminiscent of the softness of silk and velvet.
- *Watery:* Thin tea, often resulting from insufficient infusion.

AUTHORS

FABIO PETRONI was born in Corinaldo (AN) in 1964. He currently lives and works in Milan. He studied photography and later collaborated with the most established professionals in the industry. His professional career soon led him to specialize in portrait and still-life photography, in which he has developed an intuitive and rigorous style. Over the years, he has photographed prominent figures of the Italian cultural, medical, and economic scene. He works with leading advertising agencies and has created numerous campaigns for prestigious businesses and companies known around the world. Moreover, he personally handles the image of major Italian brands. For White Star Publishers, he has published *Horses: Master Portraits* (2010), *Mutt's Life!* (2011), *Cocktails, Roses*, and *Supercats!* (2012), *Orchids* and *Chili Pepper: Moments of Spicy Passion* (2013). As the official photographer of the International Jumping Riders Club (IJRC), he manages the visual communication of equestrian competitions on an international scale. Website: www.fabiopetronistudio.com

GABRIELLA LOMBARDI was born in Alexandria in 1974. She lives and works in Milan. Her university studies led her to Granada, in southern Spain, where she immersed herself in the cultural influences of the Arab world, combined with the aroma of tea enjoyed in the many "teterias" (teahouses).

It was here that she developed her passion for tea and all its rituals. Upon returning to Italy, she worked as a copywriter for some of the most famous Italian advertising agencies. After giving birth to two children, in 2010 she decided to change her life and pursue her dream by opening the *Chà Tea Atelier*. This was the first shop in Milan with a tea room specializing in the sale and tasting of fine teas. An avid traveler, she regularly journeys to China to uncover the secrets of the art of tea, furthering her knowledge and skills in the place where this extraordinary beverage originated. *Tea Sommelier* is her first book.

GIOVANNI RUGGIERI was born in Bethlehem in 1984 but grew up in Piedmont, Italy. He received professional training in Michelin-starred Italian kitchens, including Piazza Duomo in Alba and Scrigno del Duomo in Trento. As the chef at the Refettorio Simplicitas, a restaurant of refined elegance in Milan's Brera district, Ruggieri is dedicated to promoting a renewed approach to food based on simplicity and a strong emphasis on high-quality raw materials, selected according to seasonality and wholesomeness. Ruggieri prepares authentic classic dishes and flavors, featuring many niche products typical of the local territory. His cuisine is characterized by simplicity, balance, and a rustic, almost ascetic quality.

ALPHABETICAL INDEX OF TEAS

ALPHABETICAL INDEX OF NAMES

ALPHABETICAL INDEX OF RECIPE INGREDIENTS

PHOTO CREDITS

All the photographs are by Fabio Petroni, except:
page 22 Mary Evans Picture Library
image of the Chinese character cha (meaning "tea") Joey Chung/iStockphoto

Gabriella Lombardi wishes to thank Chà Tea Atelier for supplying the tea and accessories;
Salvatore Nicchi, for his valuable advice on technical aspects;
Valentina Mecchia, for her infectious optimism;
Ettore, Elena and Emma, her life companions and greatest supporters.

Fabio Petroni wishes to thank Simone Bergamaschi, photo assistant;
Cristian Ginelli, art director;
High Tech Milano for the supply of accessories.

Originally Published by WhiteStar, s.r.l.
World English language edition by Mango Publishing Group, a division of Mango Media Inc.

Cover, Layout & Design: Dataworks

For permission requests, please contact the publisher at:

Mango Publishing Group
2850 Douglas Road, 2nd Floor
Coral Gables, FL 33134 USA
info@mango.bz

For special orders, quantity sales, course adoptions and corporate sales, please email the publisher at sales@mango.bz. For trade and wholesale sales, please contact Ingram Publisher Services at customer. service@ingramcontent.com or +1.800.509.4887.

Why We Love Tea: A Tea Lover's Guide to Tea Rituals, History, and Culture

ISBN (pb) 978-1-68481-381-0 (hc) 978-1-68481-382-7 (e) 978-1-68481-383-4
LCCN: has been requested
BISAC: CKB019000, COOKING / Beverages / Coffee & Tea

Printed in the United States of America

Printed in the USA
CPSIA information can be obtained
at www.ICGtesting.com
JSHW070247041024
71003JS00007B/9